SINGER®

PERFECT

plus

**Creative Publishing
international**

First published in the United States of America by
Creative Publishing international, Inc., a member of
Quayside Publishing Group
400 First Avenue North
Suite 300
Minneapolis, MN 55401
1-800-328-3895
www.creativepub.com

ISBN-13: 978-1-58923-394-2
ISBN-10: 1-58923-394-8

10 9 8 7 6 5 4 3 2 1

Library of Congress Cataloging-in-Publication Data
Cheetham, Kathleen.
  Singer perfect plus : sew a mix-and-match wardrobe for plus and petite-plus sizes / Kathleen Cheetham.
     p. cm.
  Includes index.
ISBN-13: 978-1-58923-394-2
ISBN-10: 1-58923-394-8
  1. Machine sewing. 2. Tailoring (Women's) 3. Overweight women--Clothing. I. Title.
TT713.C54 2009
646.2'044--dc22

                                                    2008030415

Technical Editor: Jennifer Sauer
Book Design: Holtz Design
Cover Design: everlution design
Page Layout: boston page pro
Photographs: images on pages 8, 13, 60, 70, 72, 74, 80, 90, 96, 97, 98,
     102, 114, and 122 by Glenn Scott Photography
Copy Editor: Terri Autieri
Proofreader: Elaine Gross

Printed and bound in China
Patterns printed in USA

SINGER®

PERFECT *plus*

SEW A MIX-AND-MATCH WARDROBE FOR PLUS AND PETITE-PLUS SIZES

Kathleen Cheetham

Creative Publishing
international

Contents

Flirty Skirt   52

Style Options

    On the Straight of Grain

    With Sheer Overlay

    Bias Cut

Shapely Blouse   62

Style Options

    Long Sleeve

    Cap Sleeve

    Long Sleeve with Two Collar Variations

    Cap Sleeve with Two Collar Variations

    Piping

    Fast Cuff

    Button Treatments

Classic Fly-Front Pants   84

Style Options

    Comfort Side-Back Waistband

    Capri Style

    Full Elastic Waist

    Belt Loops

Simple Slimming Jacket 104

Style Options
Unlined
Lined with Facing Only
Lined with Two Collar Variations

51 Mix-and-Match Wardrobe Choices 123

Acknowledgments

WHILE WRITING THIS BOOK, I had the privilege of working with some of the finest professionals on the continent. None can compare to Vija Anca, my assistant in the studio, who was premiere in creating the beautiful garments shown in this book. My sister, Maxine Alcock, is the designer for most of the stunning jewelry pieces that accessorize our fashions. I also want to give a big thank-you to the fabulous women who modeled my garments; to Deborah Cannarella, acquisitions editor; the staff at Creative Publishing international for all of their hard work; Cecelia Podolak for showing me that a book like this is indeed doable; and to my agent, Richard Broadhead. Thanks to Sheila Wong and Betty Carlson, my office organizers, for keeping things running as they should. Finally, thanks to my family, especially my husband, Dan, who has been my inspiration and support for the last three decades.

Special thanks to these fine fabric sellers for providing many of the lovely fabrics seen in this book:

The Batik Butik, Victoria, British Columbia
www.batikbutik.com

Exotic Silks, Mountain View, California
www.exoticsilks.com

JB Silks, Surrey, British Columbia
www.jbsilks.com

The Woolen Mill Store, Portland, Oregon
http://thewoolenmillstore.blogspot.com

Télio, Montreal, Quebec
www.telio.com

Troy Corporation, Chicago, Illinois
www.troy-corp.com

Introduction

YOUR CLOSET IS FULL, but you have nothing to wear. Sound familiar? You bought this great top because it was on sale but never found anything to match. Only five pounds to lose and you were sure you could get into those pants. That jacket looked gorgeous, but the fabric is too scratchy so it hangs unworn. And this dress was stunning, but you could never find the right occasion to wear it.

Some garments don't fit, some don't match, and some just don't feel right. Some you bought for another phase of your life—a different career perhaps— and are not appropriate for the new you. In short, the woman who bought all those clothes has left the building!

Wouldn't it be nice to have a wardrobe that looks fabulous and also *works* for you? Wouldn't it be great to open the closet door and know that you have something to wear for any of the many different occasions in your life? If you sew, you have the power to create this kind of wardrobe.

In *Perfect Plus,* you'll find four basic patterns designed to fit and flatter plus and petite-plus figures: a flirty skirt, a shapely blouse, classic fly-front pants, and a simple slimming jacket. You can work with these patterns over and over again to create a mix-and-match wardrobe that works with your lifestyle and every occasion. You'll also find instructions on how to customize the garments to suit your unique style, custom-fit them for your shape, and sew them with professional results.

The most wonderful part of your new mix-and-match wardrobe is that it will continue to grow as you experiment with these four patterns and with different fabrics, textures, and colors—adding fun and interesting twists that perfectly express your signature style.

Chapter One

Who Are You Dressing?

IMAGINE HAVING a completely coordinated mix-and-match wardrobe that not only flatters your figure but fits perfectly, too.

YOUR CLOSET IS FULL, but you have nothing to wear. Nothing matches; nothing fits! The woman who bought all those clothes has changed her lifestyle, switched jobs, gained weight, lost weight—any number of things might have happened, and the clothes in the closet just don't work for her anymore. Or maybe she bought the garments for the wrong reasons. They fit or *almost* fit when she bought them, or they were on sale, or she hoped that she'd find something to go with them but never did.

The woman who owns all these clothes simply may not know who she is any longer. Women spend so much time looking after others that they forget or lose track of who they are. That's why so often the clothes that wind up in the closet don't really ever make it out of the closet.

Before spending precious time and money to sew something or buy something, you should find out just who you are. Here are some helpful tips from designers in the ready-to-wear industry.

Create Your Personal Profile

Profiling is an important first step that helps professional clothing designers and manufacturers to take stock of their customers. Before manufacturers of ready-to-wear create a collection, they identify the customers they are dressing. To do this, they create a hypothetical woman, defining her age, occupation, income, activities, and personal style.

With these characteristics in mind, the manufacturer designs a wardrobe for its hypothetical woman, referring to all the elements in the profile to decide on garment preferences, style details, fabric types, and colors. This same process is essential when planning your own wardrobe. You can create a profile in the same way a manufacturer does and ensure that you have the clothes that really work for you.

Creating your personal profile is essentially an exercise in awareness—being aware of who you are and what you do. Take some time to think about that before you answer the questions I've presented on page 10. Some questions may not seem relevant, but they are. You may have to think about some of them for a while before you can answer. Jot down your answers as they come to you, just as you would keep a shopping list. In the process of thinking and writing, many aspects of your personality, lifestyle, and wardrobe needs will come to mind.

Having a wardrobe that meets all your needs is important. Your current wardrobe may be serving only part of, or worse yet, none of your needs! Review your answers. Take note of any situations or conditions that you think are not being well served by your current wardrobe.

You especially need to analyze your wardrobe needs during periods of life transitions. For example, it's common for a mom returning to the workforce to have a closet full of casual "at-home" pieces—jeans and T-shirts—but no jackets or skirts. A recently retired woman may find herself with plenty of structured jackets but nothing to wear for her new leisurely lifestyle.

The goal here is to create the clothes that you need for the life you live now. Consider how your answers to these questions might affect the choices you make as you plan to sew your mix-and-match wardrobe. You should focus your wardrobe building on whatever you spend most of your time doing. Many of us make the mistake of spending 80 percent of our time and money on a wardrobe for activities that only occupy 10 percent of our daily lives!

Based on your answers to the questions on page 10, write down what pieces of clothing you think you need, for what aspects of your life. Describe the types of fabrics you like to wear. What colors would you like to have more of in your wardrobe? You'll refer to this list later as you choose which garments to make.

For example, I made a profile of my everyday activities, labeling them as Casual, Business Casual, Professional, Social, and Evening/Special Occasion (page 12). I also assigned an approximate time value to each activity—how much time I actually spend engaged in that activity. With this information, I am able to identify the clothing items I need for each type of activity.

Personal Profile

Photocopy this list, fill out your answers, and keep it with you for easy reference. Your answers may change over time. If so, create a new profile.

- **How do you spend your time?**

  How do you spend a typical weekday?

  _____

  What do you do in the evenings?

  _____

  How do you spend a typical weekend?

  _____

  What are your special events?

  _____

- **Where do you go?**

  Do you work at home or outside the home?

  _____

  Do you attend worship services, community functions, or meetings?

  _____

  What do you do for fun? Think of your hobbies, fitness regimen, and other types of recreation. Assign an approximate amount of time that you spend for each type of activity.

  _____

  What is the climate like where you live? How do the seasons affect your wardrobe?

  _____

- **Who do you spend your time with?**

  What are the needs of those you live with or spend time with?

  _____

  Do you have children, elderly parents, or pets?

  _____

How do these circumstances affect your wardrobe needs?

  _____

- **What are your needs?**

  Do you have special needs or health issues that play a role in your wardrobe choices?

  _____

  What do you feel comfortable wearing?

  _____

  What do you feel uncomfortable wearing?

  _____

  Do you prefer to machine-wash your clothing? Is some dry cleaning okay?

  _____

- **What's in your closet?**

  What do you keep wearing, even though it may be worn out?

  _____

  What is it about this garment that you like so much? Is it the color, the appropriateness of the style, the fact that it fits well, or the comfort of the fabric and how it feels on your skin?

  _____

- **What about color?**

  Remember back to when someone said, "You look fabulous in that color. Why don't you wear that more often?" What was that color?

  _____

  What other colors have you received compliments about?

  _____

This exercise helps me determine where I need to put the emphasis in creating my wardrobe.

Based on my profile, I can see that my greatest wardrobe need is for casual and business casual clothing. Also, because my casual events involve cooking, small children, dogs, and the outdoors, my casual garments would be best in wash-and-wear fabrics. Because I live in a cool climate with lots of rain, I like to wear pants for warmth. For casual wear, I like cotton. For business casual, I like wool in the winter and washable rayon in the summer.

For my professional, special-occasion, and evening events, I am usually away from home (and away from small children and dogs!). I like to wear soft linens, wools, silk, and novelty fibers—which all require dry-cleaning, but that's okay with me.

Of course, your profile will be unique to you. Make your own profile using the list of questions on the facing page to see where you need to focus your wardrobe attention for the life that you are living now. Then think about whether your wardrobe categories are suited—in type and proportion—to your lifestyle categories.

The Core of Your Wardrobe

Did you know that ready-to-wear manufacturers manage very nicely with only four basic patterns: skirt, blouse, pants, and jacket? They use their patterns over and over again, changing collections simply by changing fabrics, adding a little design detail, or modifying a neckline, a sleeve, or a hem—all simple but effective changes.

The four basic garments provided in this book can work for you in the same way. You can make them for casual, business casual, professional, social, or special occasions—depending on your personal profile. All you need to do is choose a fabric that is appropriate to the activity and a color that works well for you.

For example, you'll learn how you can make the same jacket pattern in corduroy to create a perfect casual look for shopping or a walk outdoors, and also in wool to create stunning business attire. Cut the pattern again in a novelty fabric for a special-occasion garment. You can make several versions of the same pattern, cutting skirts, pants, jackets, and blouses in fabrics appropriate for all of your activities—each time, making the perfect item to fit your lifestyle and your needs.

When shopping in retail stores, have you noticed that ready-to-wear designers present their collections in mix-and-match groupings? All the pieces on the rack are interchangeable. You can wear the jacket with the pants and blouse. Or, you can wear the skirt and change the blouse, and it all still works together beautifully. There are often solids, prints, and different textures, but the wardrobe is cohesive. As a sewer, you have the power to create your own interchangeable, cohesive wardrobe. In addition to using the four basic patterns, you'll find instructions for creating several design variations so you can fill your closet with many beautiful options.

Your Best Customer

Visualize this scene. A customer comes to me for a fitting and we encounter a fitting challenge. I look at her and say, "If you would lose some weight, we wouldn't be having this problem." Did your mouth drop open in shock? It's unthinkable that I would speak to a customer in this way. It's unprofessional, not to mention rude and hurtful.

We wouldn't dream of treating another person in such a disrespectful way, yet we say things like this to ourselves all the time. I'd like to invite you to think differently now. Think of yourself as the tailor and the woman you see in the mirror as your customer, your very best customer.

Let's start by having more respect for this customer and let's do a good job for her. It's your job to take good care of this lady and to see to her needs in the best way possible. The world of fashion may not have served the plus-size woman well, but, as a sewer, you have the interest and the skills to do so. You'll learn new skills, too, so you can find new ways to meet your best customer's needs—and to have fun along the way.

Personal Profile for Kathleen Cheetham

How do you spend a typical weekday?

6:30 a.m. Walk the dogs. Eat breakfast. Watch the news.
Casual, 7 ½ hours per week

8 a.m. Plan the evening meal. Do housekeeping.
Casual, 5 hours per week

9 a.m. Begin workday in studio.
1 p.m. Meet with customers.
Business Casual, 45 hours per week

6 p.m. Have dinner with family.
Casual, 10 ½ hours per week

What do you do in the evenings?

Network and participate in business meetings.
Professional, 3 hours per week

Visit with sister and girlfriends.
Casual, 3 hours per week

Work at the computer. Keep up with family correspondence.
Casual, 6 hours per week

Attend weaving guild meetings.
Casual, 3 hours per week

How do you spend a typical weekend?

WEEKENDS AT HOME:
Host family dinners.
Visit with grandchildren.
Shop bazaars and tag sales.
Garden.
Hike (forest, river, beach) with dogs and children.
Take photographs.
Casual, 6 hours per week

Attend church services.
Professional, 2 hours per week

Visit art galleries and the library.
Attend seminars.
Social, 4 hours per month

WEEKENDS TRAVELING ON BUSINESS:
Travel by air and by car.
Business Casual, 70 hours per year

Teach classes on sewing, fitting, and pattern making.
Business Casual, 100 hours per year

Emcee fashion shows.
Evening/Special Occasion, 25 hours per year

Host informational booth at trade shows.
Professional, 100 hours per year

What are your special events?

Attend weddings, baptisms, graduations, and funerals.
Social, 20 hours per year

Attend conferences and formal banquets with husband's business associates.
Evening/Special Occasion, 15 hours per year

Attend concerts, opera, and theater.
Social, 15 hours per year

Total hours spent on activities:

Next, I add up how many hours per week and then how many hours per year that I spend on each type of activity.

Casual: 41 hours per week or 2,132 hours per year

Business Casual: 45 hours per week, plus travel and teaching time away from home, or 2,510 hours per year

Professional: 360 hours per year

Social: 83 hours per year

Evening/Special Occasion: 40 hours per year

Chapter Two

Designing Your Wardrobe

THE MOST ESSENTIAL rule when choosing fabrics for your wardrobe is to choose a color that looks great on you!

THE GOAL IS TO CREATE a cohesive wardrobe, a little collection of pieces that will interchange easily and serve your lifestyle well. The cohesive wardrobe begins with a core wardrobe of two or three basic pieces: a skirt or pants and a blouse. You'll add other, coordinating pieces later.

For your first fabric, choose a neutral, solid color. The only rule is that the color must look good on you—no, not just good, fabulous! This color is at the very heart of your new wardrobe, the foundation for everything else that you will make. You'll add prints later, to link to new solids. If this first, neutral color looks fabulous on you, then every other matching or complementary color—and every garment in those colors—will look fabulous, too.

About Neutrals

A neutral color makes the best core color for your mix-and-match wardrobe. Black, beige, navy, gray, plum, brown, and white are all great choices. Before you say, "I can't wear that color," remember that neutrals are blends of more than one hue. Some of the undertone colors that create the shade are cool, and others are warm. Hold the fabric to your face and check the mirror to see if the undertone is flattering to your skin, hair, and eye coloring.

A beautiful neutral alone is not enough, however. **You must be comfortable with the texture and drape of the fabric—the overall feel of the fabric.** When you are shopping for fabric, drape it across the smooth skin on the inside of your elbow. What is your immediate reaction? What feels luscious and smooth to one woman might feel slick to another.

Keep your comfort in mind as well. A soft, curvaceous woman might not feel comfortable wearing a firm, stiff fabric. A woman with a muscular, athletic build might not feel comfortable wearing soft, flowing fabrics. **In general, soft, drapable fabrics are the best choices for a full-figured woman because they fall softly over the body's curves.**

Getting a fabric that feels right is an important step in creating an ensemble that will give you pleasure—and lead to a comfortable, confident you.

Choosing Fabrics

You'll find fabric suggestions listed for each garment pattern in the book. When creating the design, the pattern designer thinks about which fabrics will look best. Generally, you would make a blouse in a lightweight fabric, a skirt or pants in a medium-weight fabric, and jackets in a heavier fabric.

Some flattering fabrics with soft drape include jerseys, single and double knits, interlocks, chiffons, crepes, challis, georgettes, lightweight gabardines, soft denims, flannels, crepe-back satins, lightweight corduroys, and stretch velvets.

Make sure the fabric meets all the requirements in your profile (page 10). Here's a checklist of questions to ask yourself when choosing fabrics.

- ❑ Am I comfortable with the required cleaning method? Does the fabric need to be dry-cleaned or can it be hand- or machine-washed?
- ❑ Is the fabric suitable for my lifestyle and the activities specified on my profile? For example, a wool crepe jacket would be great at the office but not very practical to wear at home around small children.
- ❑ How does this fabric feel against my skin? Does it have the kind of drape that works best with my body type?
- ❑ Does the fabric suit the climate?

Cut a large swatch of each fabric you purchase. Use pinking shears to cut neat edges. You'll refer to your swatches to help you stay on track and expand your wardrobe in a planned and cohesive way.

The Core Wardrobe

You'll make two basic pieces from your neutral fabric—a core outfit—which can be either a blouse and pants or a blouse and skirt. After choosing the fabric for your first outfit, cut a swatch that is about the size of your hand. I like to make the swatch hand-sized because it is big enough to look at with accuracy. Little swatches can fool the eye and don't give you a true sense of proportion. Serge or pink the raw edges, roll the swatch up cigar-style, and store in a small resealable plastic bag. Keep the bag in your purse so you have it ready for your next shopping trip—for additional fabrics, ready-to-wear pieces, and scarves, hats, jewelry, or other fashion accessories.

> **Keep swatches together** with a safety pin. Store them in a resealable plastic bag that you can carry with you as you shop.

Next, look for a print, multicolor stripe, tweed, or checked fabric to make a bridge piece. Bridge pieces act as connectors or links between your core neutral color and new colors. The bridge piece usually has several colors in it—the core color plus others that coordinate well with it.

The coordinating colors will provide you with color choices for new fabrics and accessories. The bridge piece can be a scarf or a shawl, a blouse, a jacket, or a skirt. When choosing a bridge piece, be sure that it works well with your core outfit and suits your personal profile. Again, cut swatches so you have them for reference on your shopping trips. As you collect bridge swatches, you'll discover new colors that you can introduce into your collection.

When the Seasons Change

Work with your fabulous neutral core color even as the seasons change. For warm weather, move toward a neutral with a lighter intensity of color. For cold weather, switch to a fabric with a deeper intensity of the color.

You can also choose a color that was introduced in one of the bridge pieces and build a new collection—for a new season or activity—around this color. Remember, if the first core color looked fabulous on you, then all of the matching and complementary colors will look fabulous, too.

Neutrals are also great for stretching your wardrobe dollar. You can accessorize with jewelry, scarves, and shoes in complementary or contrasting colors to change the occasion or freshen the look of your garment.

Assembling a Wardrobe

After you have your core outfit, assembling a wonderful wardrobe is easy. Use the outfit as your foundation and expand upon it little by little. A mix-and-match wardrobe is made up of clothing that works together in beautiful harmony in every combination.

Based on my personal profile, here's an example of how just one simple core outfit—neutral gray pants and a blouse—forms the foundation of a wardrobe that can take me to the office, to business meetings, to church, to luncheons, out shopping, and out on the town for a special evening.

The Essential Combo

I chose a soft polyester crepe that looks pretty with many skin tones and ties in beautifully with my salt-and-pepper hair. The crepe has a soft, flowing, comfortable drape and a weight that is heavy enough to fall nicely and not cling to soft, full curves.

Both pieces of my core outfit are the same color. When the same color is worn on top and bottom, the visual effect is of a long fluid column, which is very flattering. The viewer's eye skims up and down the line of the outfit without interruption, and the overall effect is a slim silhouette.

Because I travel a great deal, the fiber content—easy-care, wash-and-wear polyester—suits my lifestyle. The crepe is resilient, so I can roll my garments up into a suitcase and hand-wash and drip-dry them without fear of wrinkles.

Bridge Pieces

To add interest to my essential combo, I looked for a print or multicolored stripe that would work with the neutral gray. I chose a stretch woven in a cotton-and-spandex blend. Just like the polyester crepe, this fabric is wash-and-wear, so it's easy to clean. It has a smooth fluid hand that feels good against the body.

The stripe includes the same gray that is in my neutral combo and also introduces other colors—yellow and white—that liven up the gray. Yellow is a terrific complement to gray, and I liked the way it looked with my complexion.

I bought enough fabric for a blouse. To make the most of the vertical line of stripes, I chose a pointed collar and long sleeves for this blouse. The long sleeves make this a good blouse to wear in cooler weather, and it's also appropriate for the office.

A bridge piece builds on your core color and opens up new possibilities.

This gray polyester crepe fabric has a soft drape and flattering color. The fabric will fall nicely in this rounded-collar blouse without clinging to soft body curves.

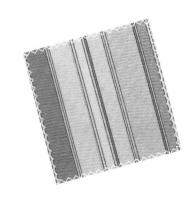

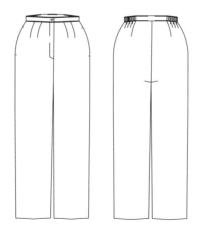

Pairing the blouse with classic fly-front pants in a matching color creates a long, fluid line.

This stripe picks up and complements the core color and adds a splash of yellow and white. The pointed collar and long sleeves of this blouse make the most of the stripes.

Why Swatches?

Swatches are the key to creating a cohesive wardrobe. Designers always carry organized sets of fabric swatches—and so should you! Have you ever bought a piece of fabric or a garment to "go with" something and after you got home found that the color was off? What a disappointment! Your little collection of swatches will ensure that you are not disappointed again. As you're shopping, you can quickly pull out your swatches to see if a garment will work with your garment collection.

Because there are so many beautiful fabrics to choose from, you can easily become overwhelmed. Your fabric swatches will also help keep you on track and focus on just those fabrics that will work with your core grouping. Salesclerks will love you, too, because they can easily lead you to just the right merchandise!

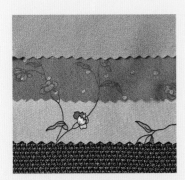

Carry your swatches with you as you shop for complementary fabrics, ready-to-wear separates, and accessories.

I added a swatch of the striped fabric to my collection and then started looking for other fabrics that include yellow or white. I found a wash-and-wear cotton/spandex fabric that is lightweight and suitable for warm weather.

This yellow fabric picks up the yellow in the striped fabric. In a cotton/spandex fabric, this cap-sleeved variation on the shapely blouse is perfect for warm weather.

I made another blouse with the same pattern, but this time with just a simple faced neckline and cap sleeves. This blouse is nice in warm weather, on its own, or worn under a jacket.

This selection of fabrics, with the neutral gray fabric as its foundation, will yield a pair of pants and three lovely blouses.

Special Occasions

When a special occasion came up on my calendar, I started looking for something a little glitzy to add to my neutral gray grouping. One quick way to transform neutral gray pants and a top into evening wear is to add a scarf or a shawl in a specialty fabric. I found a lovely piece of georgette with a smattering of sparkle. I decided to make it into a shawl that I can wear over my gray pants and blouse for an evening out (page 24).

I also found a piece of polyester stretch satin to make a flirty skirt to wear with my gray blouse. The fabric has a silky smooth hand and enough weight to skim past curves. Because it is a synthetic fabric, it is resilient, which means I can roll it up in my suitcase without worrying about wrinkles! The fabric can also be hand washed and hung to dry.

The next fabric I found is definitely a specialty piece: metallic threads, very sparkly and fluid but with a heavy hand and a nubby texture. I knew the texture would add some interest. I envisioned a jacket with which I could wear my lightweight gray crepe blouse! The blouse collar would sit outside the jacket's smooth neckline. I could wear these two pieces with either the crepe pants or the flirty satin skirt.

> **When searching for swatches,** keep texture in mind, too. Look for variety in fabric types and in the woven structure of the cloth to add interest to your garments.

This small floral print has the perfect look and feel for a flirty skirt.

A jacket in this specialty fabric—made with nubby metallic threads—is a perfect addition to my core wardrobe.

Build on the core neutral to expand the range of fabric shades, patterns, and textures.

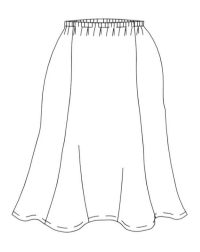

Now I have added a shawl, skirt, and jacket to my mix-and-match wardrobe and created an evening collection. Isn't it wonderful how this collection can grow to include garments for both day and evening activities—all in color-coordinated fabrics?

Changing the Season

My yellow cotton swatch led me to a cheerful cotton print. This print makes a perfect skirt to wear with my yellow cap-sleeve blouse.

Now I've got a new swatch for my collection, and this one's a dandy, full of all kinds of colors that I'll be able to build on in a spring/summer wardrobe. Working with those colors, I added a cotton/spandex blouse, lightweight corduroy pants and jacket, and stretch-woven cotton/ spandex capri pants.

My spring/summer collection is growing. Notice how pieces from the original gray core group—the striped and the yellow blouses—also work in this grouping. That's the beauty of a mix-and-match wardrobe. You have so many combinations from which to choose. Notice how the variety of color is expanding also.

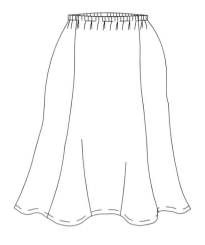

For a summery look, I made the Flirty Skirt in a colorful cotton print.

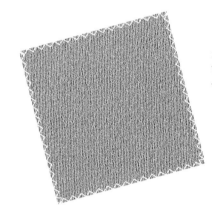

Building on the gray core colors, I have used the bridge swatches to help expand the palette of the wardrobe.

This lavender solid in cotton/spandex makes a pretty blouse to wear with the cotton print skirt.

This cheery turquoise corduroy picks up on the floral print and inspires two new pieces for the wardrobe.

This stretch-woven cotton/spandex print makes a complementary pair of capri pants for my wardrobe.

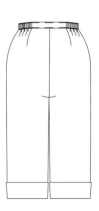

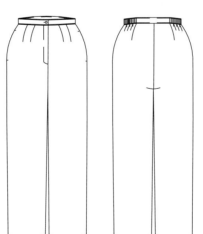

Fall/Winter Collection

The gray poly crepe blouse can be worn through the colder months, so I chose it as a base garment for my fall/winter collection. I found an understated plaid in fine wool worsted. Within its woven pattern, there are blended strands of gray, yellow, brown, blue, and white, which soften the squares in the plaid pattern and avoid creating a boxy appearance.

This plaid worsted wool fabric has a smooth hand and a lovely drape. It was easy to envision a blouse and matching skirt made in this beautiful fabric. The yellow thread running through the plaid would allow me to wear the yellow cap-sleeve blouse with it, too. I could also mix-and-match the plaid blouse and skirt with the gray crepe pants and blouse.

A plaid makes it easy to find more coordinating fabrics. Just look closely at the colors that are woven into the fabric, choose from this palette, and you can't go wrong. To add to my fall/winter collection, I decided to shop for brown and blue fabrics, the other colors in my plaid worsted.

Armed with my swatch, I found a broadcloth in soft, fawn brown worsted wool. I decided to make a pair of capri pants and a long-sleeved blouse with this fabric. To add some interest, I trimmed the blouse with piping made from the gray plaid (see page 74). For buttons, I could either pick up on the gray from the plaid or use buttons covered in plaid (see page 82).

I also found a broadcloth in warm and softly brushed blue wool—perfect for a jacket. The blue coordinates beautifully with the plaid blouse and skirt and makes a pretty contrast against the brown capri pants and the blouse.

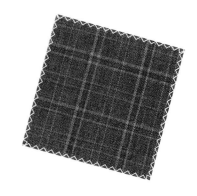

The softly contrasting colors of this plaid wool worsted will make a flattering blouse and skirt, without any danger of creating a boxy silhouette.

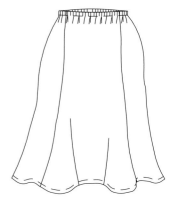

Plaid and the Full-Figured Woman

Plaids quickly introduce a number of colors into a collection, but they can be tricky for a full-figured woman to wear. The repeated rectangles or boxes in the pattern can make a woman's figure look very boxy. Here are some tricks for wearing plaid successfully.

- Use plaid in small doses—for a trim on a collar or pocket, as a covered button, or as piping.
- Cut the plaid on the bias so that the boxes in the pattern are elongated, which will eliminate the boxy look.
- Look for a plaid that has softly contrasting colors. The muted shades will downplay and soften the lines and boxes of the plaid. If the plaid is softly colored, you can easily cut your garments on the straight of grain and not get a boxy look.

This fawn brown wool picks up on the colors in the plaid worsted, inspiring a pair of capri pants and a long-sleeved blouse.

A blue wool jacket is the perfect separate to wear with four garments: the plaid blouse, the plaid skirt, the brown capri pants, and the brown blouse.

The fall/winter collection includes a plaid worsted wool that contains several soft, contrasting colors for harmonious solid fabrics.

The Perfect Accessory

A shawl is a quick-and-easy way to add an additional piece to your versatile wardrobe. It can be a lot of fun looking for, and finding, complementary fabric for your wardrobe. Look for fabric with a soft drape. Wool, silk, rayon, and polyester in challis, chiffon, charmeuse, crepe, satin, and jersey are all ideal candidates. Consider width, too. A narrow width of fabric will be well suited to a rectangular shawl. A wide width will make a luxurious square shawl that you can fold corner to corner and wear as a triangle.

To determine the length you'll need for a rectangular shawl, ask your fabric seller if you can unroll the fabric from the bolt. Drape the fabric over your shoulders until you are pleased with the length. Add an additional 2" (5 cm) for hem allowance. A square shawl should be as long as it is wide.

To make the shawl, first remove the fabric selvages, which often shrink and distort over time. Then simply hem the raw edges. If you have a serger, use your rolled-edge foot for a professional finish. Some sewing machines also have specialty attachments for rolled-edge techniques, so consult your sewing machine manual.

Consider adding a beautiful trim to make a shawl that will add extra pizzazz to your core neutrals. Trim only the short ends of a rectangular shawl. Trim the entire perimeter of a square shawl. Be sure to buy enough trim to overlap and join. Consider the weight of the trim, especially on lightweight fabrics, which might need a little weight to hang nicely. Practice applying the trim on scrap fabric first, and then create your new shawl with confidence.

The Cruise Collection

So, as you've seen, beginning with the core neutral and four basic patterns, I created a mix-and-match wardrobe of garments that span spring, summer, fall, and winter. These flattering and flexible pieces will take me to the office, meetings, church, luncheons, shopping, evenings out, and special events. I decided to add another collection that could even take me on an ocean voyage.

My brown and yellow swatches led me to a selection of washable rayon batik prints with beautiful drape. These fabrics will be cool in warm weather. I made a skirt, blouse, and unlined jacket in the rayon batiks, as shown in the photos below. The yellow cap-sleeve blouse works beautifully with both the skirt and jacket. Next, I found a stretch-woven blend of rayon and spandex, from which I made another pair of capri pants.

Working with Color

There's another way to build a colorful and flattering wardrobe. Instead of working with a fabric color as the inspiration for your collection, you can work with an inspiring object or image. Then simply search for fabric swatches that contain or are related to those colors. Fashion designers and interior designers look in many places for sources of inspiration to create a cohesive look in their clothing collections or room designs. Nature and artwork are just two of the many possible sources. Borrow their technique by exploring natural scenes and objects and works of art to create an exciting color palette for your mix-and-match wardrobe.

Inspired by Nature

Begin to look at your surroundings in a more open and appreciative way. Notice what catches your eye: colors that contrast, complement, or blend. Look for interesting textures as well.

Collect any small items that appeal to you: pebbles, shells, and driftwood from the beach; flowers and leaves from your garden. Take photographs of objects that are too big to carry home. This simple awareness can direct you to a fresh new color palette.

A photograph can provide you with plenty of ideas for colors and textures. Notice how beautifully the blue, gray, and brown work together in this top image. These beach pebbles could easily inspire a wardrobe in gray, blue, and brown.

Nature calendars are also an excellent source of inspiration. Many present reproductions of paintings, artwork, and photography, too. Find an image that you like and imagine having its colors in your wardrobe. This approach can be helpful as you browse through your fabric swatches.

The yellow in a gladiola from my garden complements this gray poly crepe fabric. A fabric in this shade would make a great blouse for a gray skirt or pants. An accessory of red or green would add interest to the ensemble.

The silk embroidery on the crepe fabric recalls the textured body of this beautiful Indian leaf butterfly. The luster of the wings inspired the blue and the gray sueded silks. The flash of orange might lead to a purse, a necklace, or earrings. (Photograph ©2001 Stephen Cole.)

Inspired by Art

When searching for color inspiration, find a painting or print that presents color in a way that appeals to your unique sensibilities. Notice the play of colors in this nineteenth-century calendar print, *La Belle Jardinière*. Can you see how you might pull the colors from this image to make a palette for a collection of garments? Some may be subdued combinations, while others may be brightly ablaze. Some colors may be very saturated or heavy, while others may be light or soft.

Think about proportions of color, too. You can use the painting or print to determine how much of each color to use in your collection. For example, notice if there are large quantities of some colors and only little dabs or flecks of others. You might consider using the small bits of color for accessories—a scarf, a purse, or a pair of earrings.

You could also invert the proportions of the colors in the image to create your color palette. For example, where the artist used a little of red and a lot of gray, you could use a lot of red and a little of gray. Have fun with the color scheme. Imagine a gray jacket with a red scarf. Then rethink the combination and imagine it as a red jacket with a gray scarf. Which combination appeals to you more?

Take your inspiration from a painting or even a calendar image, like this nineteenth-century print, *La Belle Jardinière*. Translate the color palette of the artwork into a color palette for a selection of fabrics—from soft grays to rich autumn hues. (Snark / Art Resource, NY)

You don't have to use all the colors in the painting or print you choose. Instead, isolate just one section and pull a few colors from that area to create an interesting color palette.

Cotton swatches 1

Cotton swatches 2

Silk swatches 1

Silk swatches 2

These casual fabrics (cotton swatches 1) are all cotton-based and easy to care for. The swatches include twill, fleece, broadcloth, and knit. To increase interest, add textures and novelty weaves. You don't have to sew something from each swatch—instead, keep some for reference as you shop for ready-to-wear garments. One could lead you to a perfect little knit top to add to this casual group.

In the next group of swatches (cotton swatches 2), the print encapsulated many of the colors I found in a favorite painting. I chose the remaining swatches to coordinate with the print to create a grouping for a casual wardrobe.

The solid swatches of silk (silk swatches 1) came first—again inspired by a painting. I found the embroidered silk dupioni and tweed later. The silk tweed (which would make a nice jacket) completes the grouping.

With this group of silk swatches (silk swatches 2), I experimented with a whimsical print and various weaves. Although I am working with the same colors as in my other groupings, the theme of the dressy wardrobe made with these fabrics will be completely different because of the print and textures chosen.

Chapter Three

Getting Ready to Sew

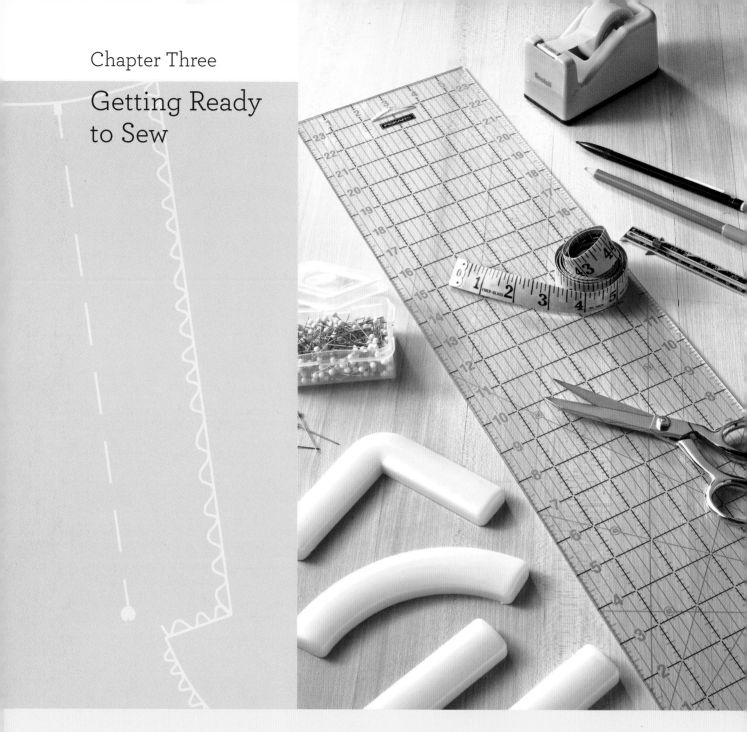

BEFORE YOU BEGIN to sew, check your body and pattern measurements. Then make an action plan (page 32). The sewing process will be faster and smoother—and you'll be sure to get a perfect fit.

SEWERS OFTEN SAY they don't have time to accomplish their sewing projects. With our full lives, little time is left at the end of each day to even set up a sewing area, never mind to work on a project! Here's some advice. Approach your sewing project as a manufacturer approaches mass production: Create an action plan (page 32). You'll accomplish more than you ever thought possible! This strategy is particularly helpful if you plan to make several pieces in a color grouping. Do the preparatory tasks in the evenings, after work. By the weekend, you'll be ready to sit down and sew your wardrobe!

You'll also save time—and get much better results—if you take some careful body measurements before you begin laying out and cutting your pattern. Follow these simple guidelines for comparing your body measurements to the pattern measurements and making the adjustments. Not only will the sewing process be easier—from start to finish—but you'll also be sure to get a perfect fit.

Working with Measurement Charts

No two people are built exactly the same way. That's why there are instructions for custom fitting included with each pattern. Compare your actual body measurements to those on the Body Measurement Chart on page 33. The chart provides the body measurements that the enclosed patterns were drafted to fit. Compare your measurements with these to determine what size garment to cut.

All the sizes from 14 to 24 are on one pattern tissue so that you can easily customize for variations in circumference. For differences in length, the pattern tissue has shorten/lengthen lines in all the appropriate places. Check the Body Measurement Chart and the Finished Garment Measurements Chart included with the enclosed pattern instructions to determine if you need to lengthen or shorten the pattern for your height. If you need to lengthen, multiply the increase in length by two to calculate the additional fabric needed for your garment.

If you need to make fitting adjustments, plan some additional time for this important process. Follow the guidelines presented in this chapter and make sure that you are happy with the fit before you cut your fabric.

Extra Fabric

To avoid problems with shrinkage, ask your fabric seller what the expected shrinkage is in your fabric choice. If the answer is 10 percent, then add an extra 10 percent to the yardage (meterage) shown in the Fabric Requirements Chart included with each pattern. Before you cut your fabric, pretreat it in the same way that you plan to clean it later. For example, if you plan to machine-wash and -dry your final garment, machine-wash and -dry the entire length of fabric before cutting.

If the fabric has a repeated design motif, such as horizontal stripes, you'll need to cut the pattern pieces to align the elements at the garment seams. Generally, a repeated horizontal print is not the most flattering choice for a full-figured woman—but if you are absolutely in love with a fabric that will need matching, plan to buy additional length. The amount depends on how large the "repeat" is. Ask your fabric seller for assistance.

Sewing Action Plan

Follow this sewing action plan to make the process easier. You'll be surprised at how much you can get done—and how quickly you can build your mix-and-match wardrobe!

Monday

Pretreat the fabrics.

One great advantage of sewing for yourself is that you can eliminate shrinkage before you sew—rather than being disappointed after the garment's first washing. If you're working with fabrics that you plan to wash, preshrink the fabric by machine-washing and -drying the yardage *before* you cut out your garment pieces. Many sewers steam-press wool and silk to preshrink them.

Remember to preshrink your interfacing, too. Simply dip the entire length of interfacing into a basin of lukewarm water. Then roll it up in a big bath towel to remove excess water, and drape it over a shower rod to dry. You won't ever have to deal with puckered facings and collars.

Tuesday

Prepare the patterns for cutting.

Preparing your patterns for cutting can be as simple as opening the envelope and lightly pressing the tissue to remove any wrinkles. For clarity, trace your size lines onto the multisize pattern with a highlighter.

Wednesday

Cut the garment pieces.

Find a good surface for cutting. If you have a well-laid-out sewing room, wonderful! Many people just clear off the dining room table, and others spread their fabric out on the floor (ouch!). One inventive sewer I know keeps a bi-fold door stored under her bed for cutting fabric. Whatever your area for cutting, be sure to clip all notches and place all construction marks onto the wrong side of your fabric.

Thursday

Interface.

Cut the interfacing pieces as indicated on the pattern. Get out your iron and ironing board, and fuse the interfacing to all garment pieces that require it.

Friday

Prepare your sewing area.

Thread your sewing machine and serger. Set up the iron, ironing board, and a clean work surface on which to lay your garment pieces. Make sure that you have all your sewing tools ready—scissors, pins, measuring tape, and fabric marker.

Saturday & Sunday

Get sewing!

Follow the sewing instructions in the given sequence. You will save time and be delighted with the professional finish of your garment. Above all, have fun throughout the process!

Body Measurement Chart

SIZE	14		16		18		20		22		24	
	in	*cm*	*in*	*cm*	*in*	*cm*	*in*	*cm*	*in*	*cm*	*in*	*cm*
High bust	36	91.5	38	96.5	40	101.5	42	106.5	44	112	46	117
Full bust	40	101.5	42	106.5	44	112	46	117	48	122	50	127
Waist	32	81.5	34	86.5	36	91.5	38	96.5	40	101.5	42	106.5
Tummy	43	109	45	114.5	47	119.5	49	124.5	51	129.5	53	134.5
Full hip	42	106.5	44	112	46	117	48	122	50	127	52	132
Back waist length	14¼	36	14⅜	36.5	14½	37	14⅝	37	14¾	37.5	14⅞	37.5
Back shoulder width	14½	37	14¾	37.5	15	38	15¼	38.5	15½	39	15¾	40

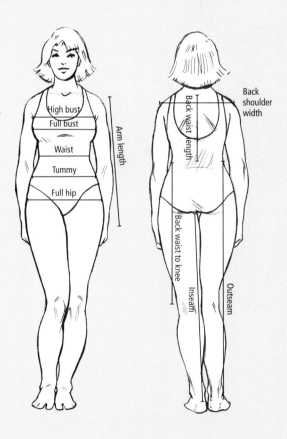

High bust — Wrap the measuring tape snugly around your chest at the armpit level.

Full bust — Wrap the measuring tape around your bust at the fullest point.

Waist — Measure the circumference of your waist.

Tummy — Measure your circumference. The fullness of the tummy is 4½" (11.5 cm) below the waist in these patterns.

Full hip — Measure your circumference. The hip fullness is 8" (20.5 cm) below the waist in these patterns.

Back waist length — Measure from the prominent bone at the base of your neck straight down to your waist.

Back shoulder width — Measure from the prominent bone at the top of one arm straight across the back to the prominent bone at the top of the opposite arm.

NOTE: For some garments, you will also need arm length, back waist to knee, inseam, and outseam measurements. See the Finished Garment Measurement Charts on pages 134–137.

About These Patterns

The patterns in this book are multisize, from size 14 to 24. A multisize pattern makes it easy to create a custom size for yourself if, for example, you are one size on the top and another on the bottom—and even if you are one size in the back and another in the front.

The patterns contain the cutting lines for six sizes and also include a seam allowance of ⅜" (1 cm). This amount of seam allowance is a ready-to-wear standard; it's also a great time and fabric saver, as it eliminates the need for trimming and clipping excess fabric during the construction process.

Bust Cup and Tummy

The patterns have been drafted for a D-cup bust and a fuller tummy.

Bust: If the difference between your full bust and high bust (chest) measurement is more than 4" (10 cm), follow the instructions for Bust Adjustments on pages 46–48.

Tummy: Plus-size women commonly have a tummy measurement that is fuller than their hip measurement. These patterns allow for a slightly fuller measurement in the tummy. You can make further adjustments by referring to Quick Fit for Pants on page 50.

Height

All the patterns are drafted for a height of 5' 2" (157.5 cm). You'll find shorten/lengthen lines on the patterns in all the appropriate places so you can customize for your height. Remember that the body is made up of distinct sections. The upper body, hip, and legs all must be considered individually when adjusting a pattern for height.

Choosing Your Size

Take your measurements accurately and honestly. Write them down in the same order in which they are listed in the Body Measurement Chart on page 33. Then compare your measurements to the chart. On the pattern, with a highlighter pen, identify the size you need to fit each section of your body. Take advantage of the pattern's multisize format to taper from one size to another as needed for your bust, waist, tummy, and hip measurements.

Blouses and Jackets

Choose your size based on your high-bust (chest) measurement to ensure a fit that's in keeping with your overall frame. Working with this measurement will eliminate the problem of making a garment that is too big in all the wrong places to accommodate a full bust. The patterns are drafted for a D-cup bust, which is equal to a full-bust measurement that is 4" (10 cm) larger than the high-bust measurement. If your full bust is either smaller or larger than a D-cup, refer to the instructions on pages 46–48 to customize the pattern to your figure.

Pants and Skirts

Choose your size according to your hip or your tummy measurement, whichever is most in keeping to your body's overall frame. If you have a fitting challenge—for example, an extra-full tummy or seat—refer to the instructions in the sidebar or text on page 50. To avoid making a garment that is too big in all the wrong places. Choose a smaller size, and add fullness in the specific areas as you need it.

Length Adjustments

Begin customizing the pattern by adjusting the length of the pattern to your own body's length measurements. Every woman's body is unique, not just in circumference, but in the way that her length is distributed through the sections of her body. Two people of the same height will differ in length from the neck to the waist, from the waist to the crotch depth, and from the crotch depth to the feet. Take note of how your body's sections differ in length from the pattern and adjust accordingly by working with the pattern's shorten/lengthen lines.

Back Waist Length

Measure the back waist length from the prominent bone at the base of the neck straight down the center back (CB) to the waistline. Keep this measurement as straight as possible from neck to waist and avoid curving over any humps. (If you have a curve or a hump in your upper back, refer to page 45.) Compare your back waist length to the chart. Whatever amount you add to or take away from the length of the back pattern piece, you must also add to or take away from the front pattern piece.

Crotch Depth

The crotch depth measurement is the length of the side seam between the waist and the crotch. Usually, this measurement is taken while the person is seated, but I find that plus-size women often experience some distortion taking the measurement that way.

Instead, tie a string around your waist and another string around your upper thigh, where you want the crotch line of your pants to fall. Stand straight and ask a sewing buddy to measure from the string at your upper thigh straight up along the side seam, over the curve of your hip, to the string at your waist.

Compare your crotch depth measurement to the Crotch Depth Chart for your size. If your crotch depth measurement differs from the chart measurement, adjust the length as needed, working with the shorten/lengthen lines on the front and back pattern pieces.

Crotch Depth Chart

Size	in	cm
14	9⅜	24
16	9⅝	24.5
18	9⅞	25
20	10⅛	25.5
22	10⅜	26.5
24	10⅝	27

Leg Length

The outseam is measured from the waist along the side seam to the finished hem. Compare your outseam length to the measurement in the Finished Garment Measurements Chart included with the pattern. Lengthen or shorten the pattern as needed. Also, keep in mind that if you make an adjustment to the crotch depth it will affect the outseam length, so you'll need to adjust accordingly.

Finished Garment Measurements

For each pattern refer to the Body Measurement Chart (page 33) and the Finished Garment Measurements Chart (pages 134–137) to ensure that the outseam, sleeve, back waist length, and hem lengths are right for you.

You need to adjust the length of both the front and back pattern pieces equally, or the side seams will not meet correctly.

To adjust the length of a pattern section, cut along the shorten/lengthen lines. Work with a ruler to add or subtract the length needed to make the pattern section the correct length for your body.

If you need to lengthen, add tissue paper as a pattern extension, as shown in this photo.

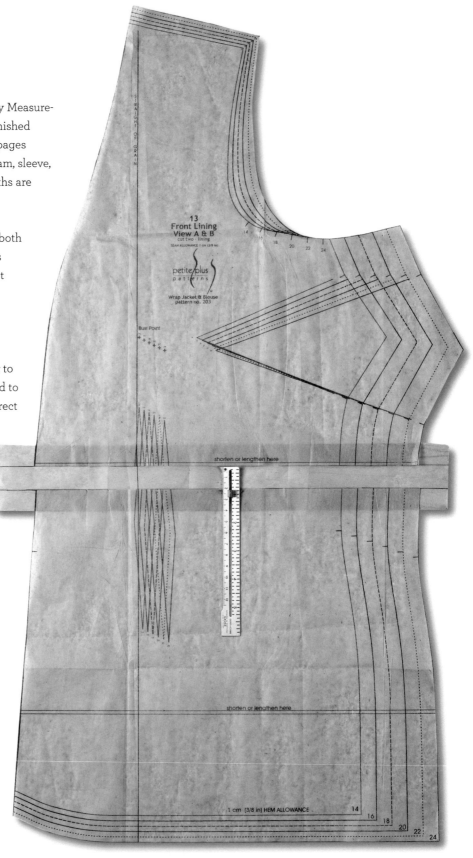

To shorten, cut the pattern tissue along the shorten/lengthen lines. Overlap the tissue to take up the required amount, checking the straight-of-grain line to ensure accuracy, as shown in this photo.

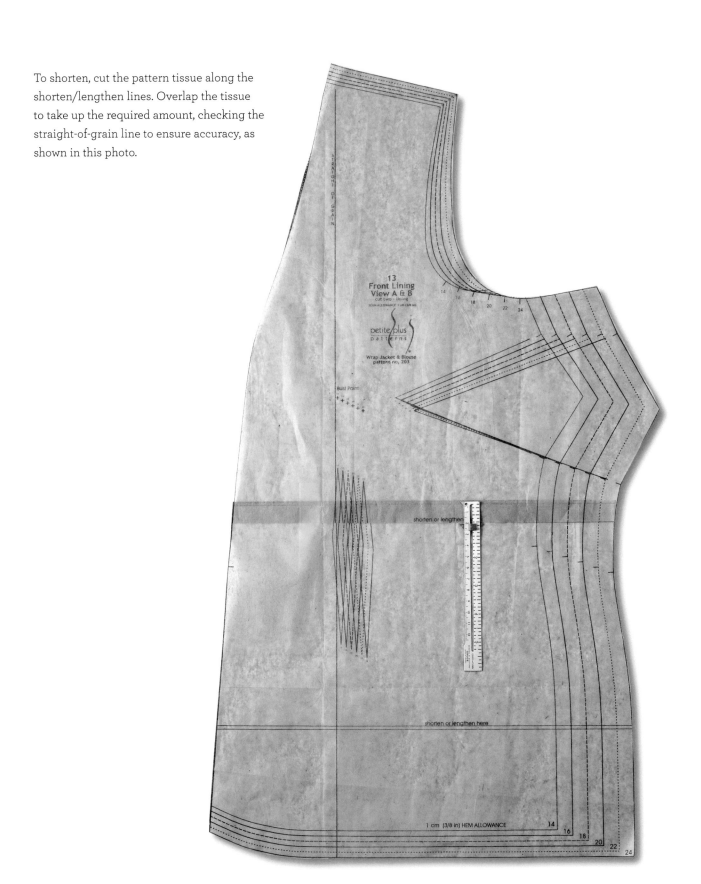

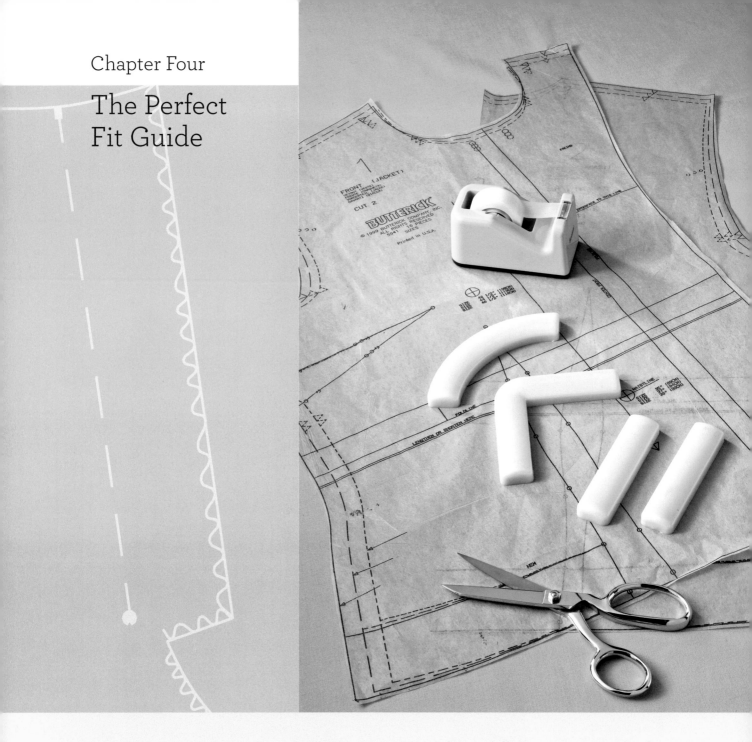

Chapter Four

The Perfect
Fit Guide

WHAT GOOD IS a beautifully sewn garment if it doesn't
fit well? To test the fit of a new pattern—before cutting the
fashion fabric—some sewers make a quick trial garment,
called a muslin, from a less expensive fabric. Cotton
broadcloth is a good fabric for a quick-fit muslin.

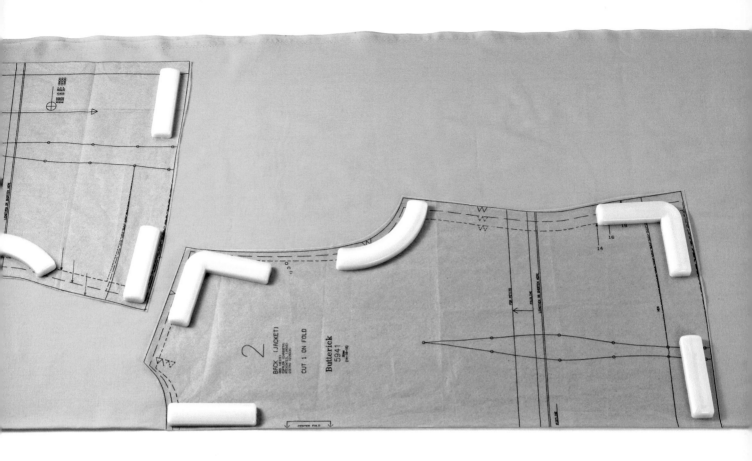

IF YOU HAVE ONLY a few pattern adjustments to make, you don't need to make a muslin, but, if you have many fit adjustments, you might want to get together with a sewing buddy and make a weekend of fine-tuning your patterns. This muslin will tell you if you need to make any additional fitting tweaks and will help you determine how much to adjust before cutting into your fashion fabric.

The muslin-making process should be quick but accurate. Instead of working with pins, I lay out the pattern on the fabric with pattern weights, as shown in the photo above. Cut only the front and the back pattern pieces, and sleeves, if your pattern has them. Don't worry about facings, pockets, and collars. You just want to see how the garment fits and whether you'll need adjustments. You can adjust the smaller pattern pieces later, based on the changes made to the larger pieces. For fitting purposes, adding an extra seam allowance along the waist edge or at any closure seams is a good idea. Be sure to mark how much extra seam allowance you are adding.

To save time, sew your muslin with a long machine stitch rather than hand basting. The machine stitch guide also helps you keep the seam allowances accurate.

When evaluating your quick-fit muslin, look for the obvious. Start at the top of the body and work downward. Having a sewing buddy evaluate the fit along your back helps, as the garment tends to distort if you need to turn to look in a mirror. When you're ready to start your fine-tuning, refer to this chapter for some fast fixes.

Shoulders

There are two quick fixes for shoulders. The first is for broad or narrow shoulders; the second is for sloping or square shoulders. Is it possible to have a combination of these shapes? Yes. Do one adjustment at a time. Make your cuts in the same place on both front and back shoulder seams and make identical adjustments to both the front and the back pattern pieces.

Broad or Narrow Shoulders

For the blouse: Cut a box from each of the front and the back shoulders. Place a sheet of pattern tracing paper behind the pattern. Draw a horizontal guideline that extends from the pattern onto the tracing paper. For wide shoulders, slide the box out along the guideline. For narrow shoulders, slide the box in. Your quick-fit muslin will provide you with the information as to how much to adjust.

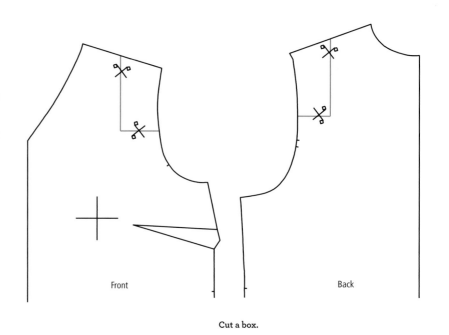

Front   Back

Cut a box.

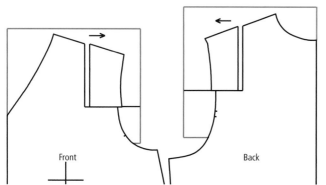

Front   Back

Slide the box out for broad shoulders.

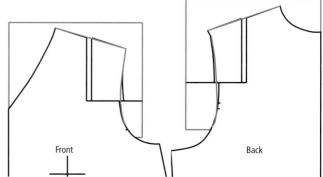

Front   Back

Redraw the cutting lines to smooth the curves.

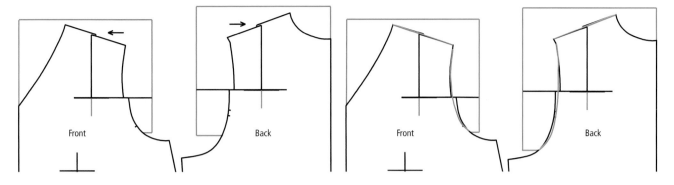

Slide the box in for narrow shoulders.

Redraw the cutting lines to smooth the curves.

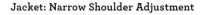

Jacket: Narrow Shoulder Adjustment

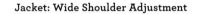

Jacket: Wide Shoulder Adjustment

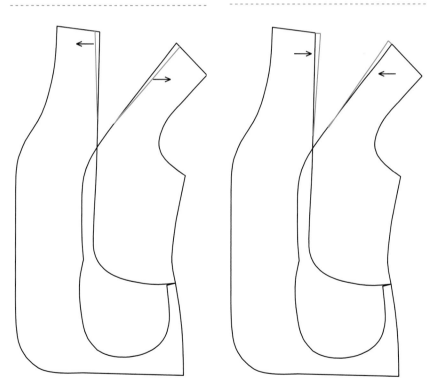

Trim the pattern tissue to
eliminate excess width.

Add tissue paper to widen by the
adjusted amount.

For the jacket: You can make easy shoulder-width adjustments along the princess seams, which continue all the way to the shoulder. Try on the jacket muslin. For narrow shoulders, pin the excess width out along the seams. For broad shoulders, open the seams until the shoulder sits the way you like it. Measure the results of your adjustments—whether you're taking in or letting out. Transfer your measurements to the pattern pieces along the princess seams, blending the line into the original seam above the bust.

Square and Sloping Shoulders

To fix a shoulder problem, you might be tempted to simply add a little or take a little from the shoulder point at the armhole. Don't do it! If you do, you'll affect the armhole circumference and the fit of the sleeve. Instead, cut an L-shape from both the front and the back pattern pieces. For square shoulders that sit high, slide the L-shape up. For sloping shoulders that slant low, slide the L-shape down. Reconnect the neck point to the shoulder point with a straight line.

Adjustments for Square and Sloping Shoulders

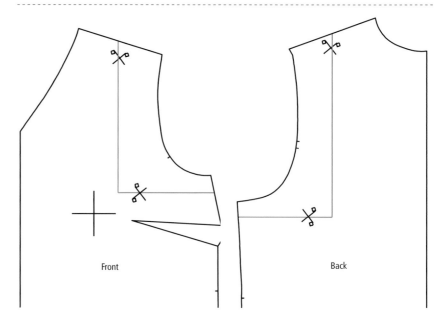

Front

Back

Cut an L-shape in the front and back.

Square Shoulders

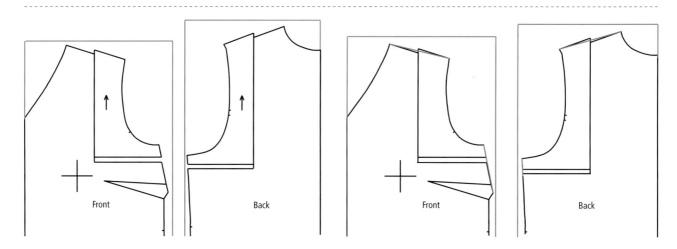

Front

Back

Front

Back

Slide the L-shapes up.

Redraw the cutting lines along the shoulder and side seams.

Sloping Shoulders

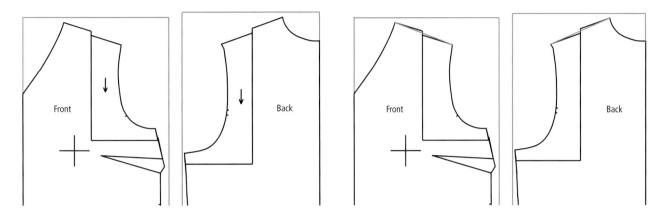

Front

Back

Front

Back

Slide the L-shapes down.

Redraw the cutting lines along the shoulder and side seams.

Adjustment for Full Upper Arms

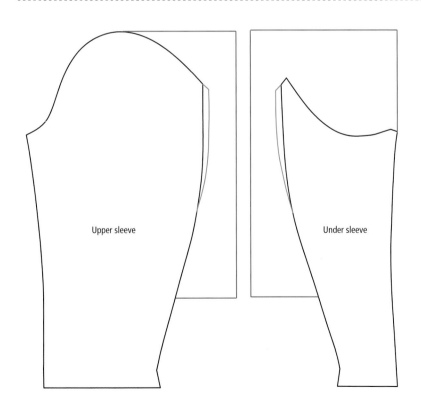

Upper sleeve

Under sleeve

Full Upper Arms

Both the blouse and jacket patterns have a two-piece sleeve, which makes it easy to add room without making the entire sleeve big and baggy. Add a little extra width by drawing a curved line along the back sleeve seam, diminishing into the original seam at the elbow. You will have a small amount of extra fabric to ease in to the armhole.

Slashing and Pivoting

Many fitting adjustments involve cutting and opening the pattern to either allow for or take away excess fabric from a specific area. The process called "slash and pivot" requires a pivot point, which works like a door hinge where the pattern separates and opens. Keep the pivot point tiny and your pattern paper will stay smooth and flat as you pivot the piece. Pattern tissue is delicate and easily torn, so place a small piece of transparent adhesive tape on the pivot point before you cut. The tape will give your little hinge of paper more resilience.

1. From outside the armscye, clip inward. Stop at the seam allowance.

2. Cut the tissue up from the hem to the bust point and then cut to the armscye. When you reach the armscye, stop at the seam allowance. Leave a little hinge that measures about ¹⁄₁₆" (2 mm). Working with a small, reinforced pivot point, you can swing the pattern open smoothly with no buckles or bumps.

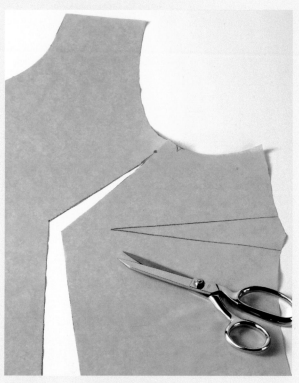

Cut up from hem.

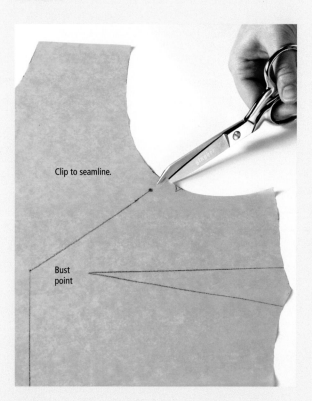

Clip to seamline.

Bust point

Full Upper Back

Many of us have rounding in the upper back and neck. Our computer-based lifestyles, genetics, or perhaps the process of aging all might contribute to this effect. Often women wear garments a size or two too large just to reduce the pulling in the neck and upper back, but the result is a garment that is too big in all the wrong places. Instead of choosing a larger garment, make this simple adjustment, which adds the room just where you need it.

Measure the high point of your rounded area and draw a horizontal line at that point across the back pattern piece. Cut with scissors to slash a line from the center back (CB) to, but not through, the armhole. Then cut from the middle of the shoulder down to the horizontal slash line. Lift the upper back.

Open the shoulder slash and pull the upper back section down until the CB line is straight again. The shoulder opening can be eased, gathered, or closed with a dart. If you choose to close the shoulder with a dart, draw the stitching line so that the point of the dart will sit one-half to two-thirds down along the length of the slash.

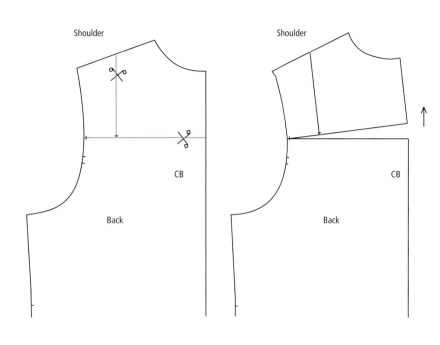

Cut from CB to, but not through, armhole.

Lift the upper back.

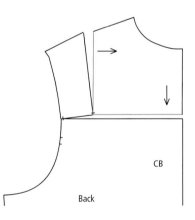

Open the shoulder slash and pull the upper back down to equalize the space.

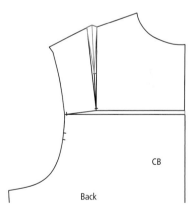

Draw the stitching lines for the shoulder dart and extend the CB line to the neck.

Gaping Neckline

Necklines that fall open, exposing more than we care to show, are easy to fix. On your muslin, pin out the excess, forming a dart from your neckline toward your bust point. Transfer this measurement to your pattern by first cutting the pattern from the neckline to the bust point. Then cut from the center of the bust dart at the seam to the bust point. Leave a little hinge of pattern paper for pivoting. Close the neckline dart. The bust dart opens a little as it takes up the extra fabric removed from the neckline. Sew the bust dart along its original sewing lines.

Bust Adjustments

For the jacket, you can make easy bust adjustments along the princess seams. Simply try on the jacket muslin, and, for a flatter bust, pin the excess fullness out along the princess seams. For a fuller bust, open the princess seams until the fabric falls smoothly with no strain. Measure and transfer this information to your pattern pieces.

The blouse pattern is drafted to fit a bust that is 4" (10 cm) fuller than the high bust or chest. If your full bust is larger or smaller than a D-cup, make an adjustment only to the front of the pattern.

For a fuller bust

For a fuller bust in the blouse, cut a line from the hem of the garment to your bust point and then to, but not through, the armhole. To accommodate a fuller bust, swing the side of the pattern out until the pattern tissue at the bust point is open to the following measurements:

DD cup	⅜"	1 cm
DDD cup	¾"	2 cm
E cup	1⅛"	3 cm
F cup	1½"	4 cm

Place a pattern weight on the upper section of the pattern or secure the pattern to the work surface with adhesive tape. Notice that the pattern has swung open widely at the hem edge. If you also have a very full abdomen, the good news is that you have already made the fitting adjustment you need for this situation. If not, you'll want to close the wide opening.

To close the opening, cut a line through the bust dart all the way to, but not through, the remaining tissue. Leave a hinge of paper for pivoting. Swing the lower section back toward the center front (CF) until it is closed

Adjustments for Gaping Neckline

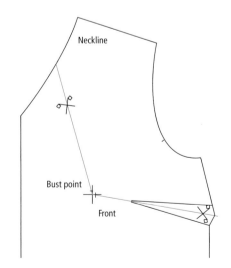

As you cut, leave a little hinge of paper at the bust point.

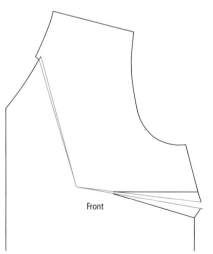

Overlap the tissue to eliminate the gaping. As you do, the bust dart opens.

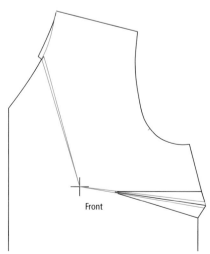

Redraw the neckline to form a smooth curve.

Find Your Bust Point

Any bust adjustment must work with your specific bust point, the fullest point of your bust, so the final dart will be positioned correctly and the fullness will be exactly where you need it.

Mark your bust point on the pattern paper. Pin the back and front shoulder pieces together as they would be sewn. Hold the pattern as it would be worn, with the center front (CF) at the center of your body. Mark an X on the pattern at your bust point.

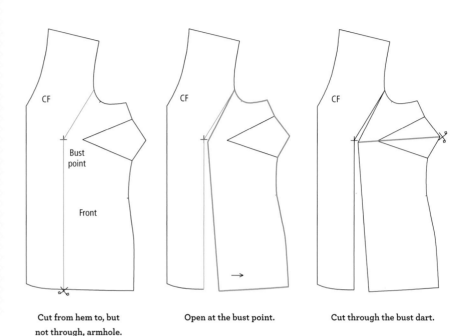

Cut from hem to, but not through, armhole.

Open at the bust point.

Cut through the bust dart.

at the hemline. Cut the CF section at bust-point level, and slide the pattern down evenly until the hemlines meet.

Redraw the dart. You'll work with the original dart legs. Just make sure that your sewing lines taper toward the bust point. Notice that the sewn dart does not extend all the way to the bust point—it's at least 1" (2.5 cm) away from it. Refer to Bust Dart Stitching on page 48.

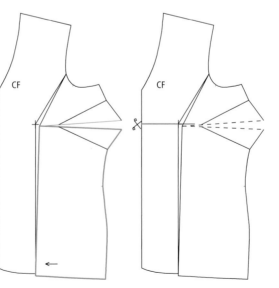

Close the pattern at hem.

Cut horizontally from the CF to the bust point.

Slide the lower front section down until the hem edges are even. Redraw the bust dart.

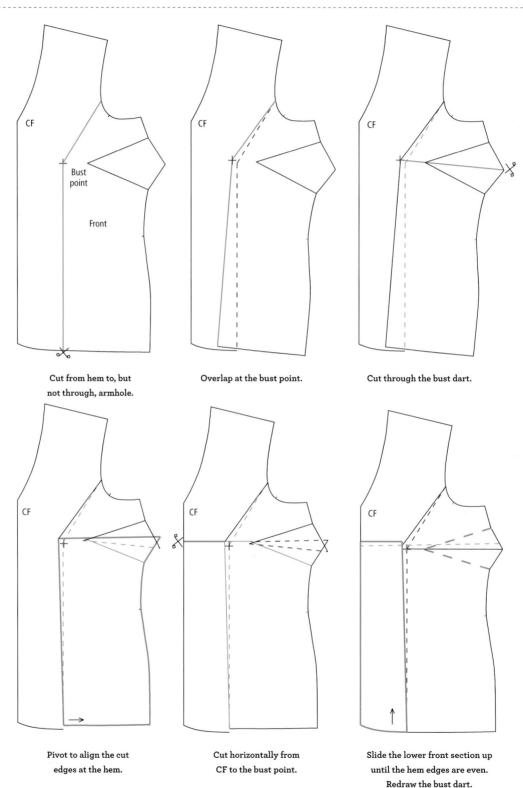

Cut from hem to, but
not through, armhole.

Overlap at the bust point.

Cut through the bust dart.

Pivot to align the cut
edges at the hem.

Cut horizontally from
CF to the bust point.

Slide the lower front section up
until the hem edges are even.
Redraw the bust dart.

For a flatter bust

For a flatter bust in the blouse, cut a line from the hem to your bust point and then to, but not through, the armhole. Overlap the pattern tissue at the bust point by the following amounts:

A cup	1⅛"	3 cm
B cup	¾"	2 cm
C cup	⅜"	1 cm

Place a pattern weight on the upper section of the pattern, or secure the pattern to the work surface with transparent tape. You will notice that the pattern has swung closed at the hem edge. Cut a line through the bust dart all the way to, but not through, the remaining tissue. Leave a little hinge of paper for pivoting. Swing the lower section away from the center front (CF) until it touches at the hemline. Notice that the bust dart has become much smaller. Finally, cut the CF section at bust-point level, and slide the pattern up evenly until the hemlines meet.

Redraw the dart. You'll work with the original dart legs. Make sure that your sewing lines taper toward the bust point.

Skirt Hem Adjustments

A dipping hem—one that is long in the front and short in the back or vice versa—is a common problem with skirts. Here's an easy solution. Before completing the waist treatment, try on the skirt, and hold it in place with a length of narrow elastic around your waist. Now pull up the skirt until the hem sits evenly. Mark the waist with pins or a fabric marker. Remove the skirt, and trim off the uneven excess at the waist. Finish the waist treatment, and your skirt hem will hang perfectly even.

Bust Dart Stitching

The fuller the bust, the farther back the finished dart point should sit, to allow more ease. For a smaller bust, the dart point must be closer to the bust point to remove excess fabric from the bust area. When adjusting for fuller or flatter bust points, follow these guidelines for determining how far the sewn dart point should be from the bust point.

A cup
1" (2.5 cm) from bust point

B or C cup
1½" (4 cm) from bust point

D or DD cup
2" to 2½" (5 to 6.5 cm) from bust point

E or F cup
3" to 3½" (7.5 to 9 cm) from bust point

Dipping Hem Adjustment

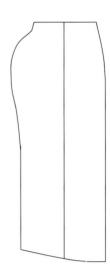

Try on skirt and raise the waist to even the hem.

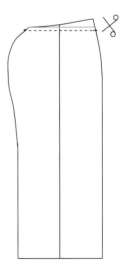

Trim off uneven excess at the waist.

Quick Fit for Pants

Most of us have what some might call disproportionate bodies—for example, a flat seat but a full tummy or a full seat and a flat tummy. Multisize patterns are wonderful to work with for this very reason. You can resolve many fitting problems just by cutting the garment back in one size and the front in another. For example, with a flat seat and a full tummy, you might cut a size 14 back and a size 16 or 18 front for your pants.

When working with a different-size back and front, be consistent with the length of your side seams. With a highlighter pen, outline your preferred cutting lines. Next, decide on your waistline position. Check that all the pattern notches on the front and back pieces match. Choose the pocket notches that correspond to your preferred waist position. Be sure to also mark the waistband to agree with your multisize adjustment.

Pants Adjustments

In addition to length, there are typically two common problem areas when it comes to fitting pants. The seat measurement is either too narrow or too wide for your figure. Here are quick ways to address both situations.

For a fuller seat

If you need more room in the seat, cut across the seat of the pattern from the center back (CB) to, but not through, the side seam. Leave a little hinge of paper for pivoting. Then lift the upper section of the pattern. This adjustment will offer more length to cover the seat—helpful if your pants tend to pull down when you sit. Redraw the CB cutting line, connecting the waistline to the crotch shelf line.

Extend the back crotch shelf line, drawing a fuller back inseam. This back inseam line can be straight, curved inward, or curved outward, depending on the fullness of your inner thighs. This adjustment is also helpful if you have excessive cupping and pulling under the seat.

For a flatter seat

To eliminate bagginess in the back leg and seat, cut across the seat of the pattern from the center back (CB) to, but not through, the side seam. Leave a little hinge of paper for pivoting. Then drop the upper section of the pattern. This adjustment will reduce the length of fabric covering the seat, just what you need if you feel that just pulling up a handful of fabric will make the pants fit more smoothly. Redraw the CB cutting line. You will lose a little width and will need to scoop slightly at the curve.

You can also reduce the width of the back leg by repositioning the crotch point and drawing a narrower back inseam. This back inseam line can be drawn straight, curved inward, or curved outward, depending on the fullness of your inner thighs. This adjustment is helpful if you have excessive fabric under the seat along the back leg.

Fuller Seat Adjustment

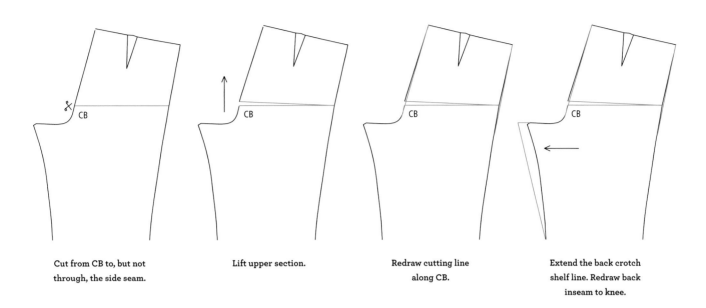

Cut from CB to, but not through, the side seam.

Lift upper section.

Redraw cutting line along CB.

Extend the back crotch shelf line. Redraw back inseam to knee.

Flatter Seat Adjustment

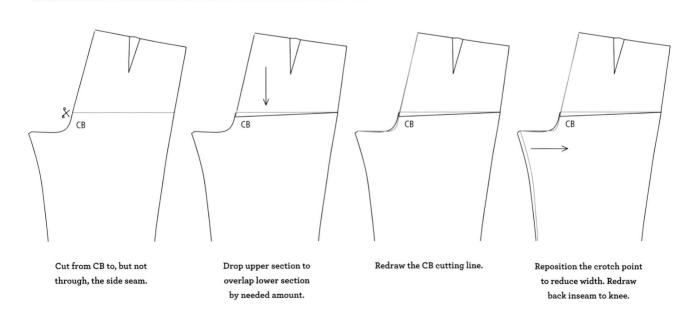

Cut from CB to, but not through, the side seam.

Drop upper section to overlap lower section by needed amount.

Redraw the CB cutting line.

Reposition the crotch point to reduce width. Redraw back inseam to knee.

Flirty Skirt

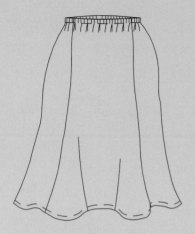

THIS IS THE SIMPLEST, fastest skirt you will ever make! It's also a sexy, flirty style that will smooth over your curves. It's so fast and easy to make, you'll want to make several—in a wide array of fabrics to suit the many different types of occasions and activities in your life. Mix and match the Flirty Skirt with long- and short-sleeve blouses, lined and unlined jackets, and even your perfect shawl (page 24) to create fun and feminine outfits that will take you from everyday casual to glamorous.

Flirty Skirt in stretch satin print, with poly crepe blouse (page 62) and a sparkly georgette shawl (page 24)

Flirty Skirt in a cotton blend print, worn with cotton blouse
(page 62) and corduroy jacket (page 104)

Flirty Skirt in rayon batik, worn with matching blouse (page 62)

Suggested Fabric Layout for All Sizes

Here are the suggested fabric layouts for your pattern pieces to make the most efficient use of the fabric and position the pieces as needed on the fabric grain. Please note the suggested width of the fabric, and also whether the fabric is folded or single ply.

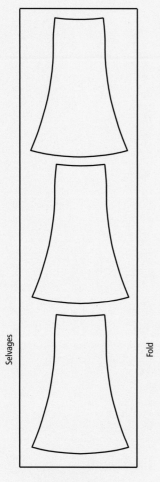

Cut on the straight of grain
Fabric width: 45" to 60" (115 to 150 cm)

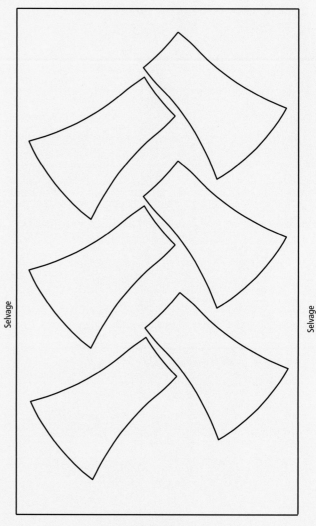

Cut on the bias
Fabric width: 54" to 60" (140 to 150 cm)
Fabric is single ply.

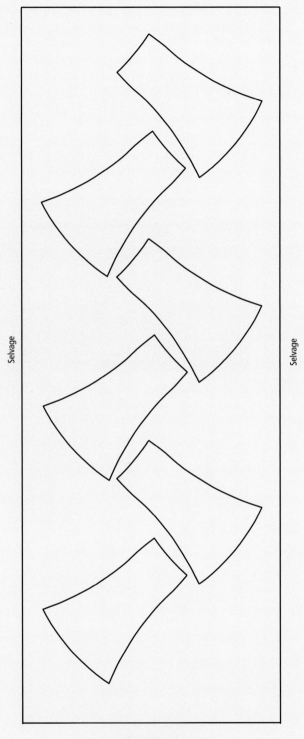

Selvage

Selvage

Cut on the bias
Fabric width: 45" (115 cm)
Fabric is single ply.

Custom Fitting

Compare your own measurements to the Body Measurement Chart (page 33) and review the Finished Garment Measurements Chart (page 134). Make a note of any necessary adjustments.

It's always a good idea to make a quick-fit muslin when making a new pattern (page 39). When you've made the muslin, evaluate the fit. If you think the skirt pattern needs tweaking, follow the helpful advice in The Perfect Fit Guide chapter (pages 38–51).

Fabric and Notions

Refer to the layouts on pages 54–55 and the fabric requirements on page 134. Depending on the season and the occasion, choose woven or knit fabrics with a soft drape in wool, cotton, silk, rayon, or polyester.

Step 1   With right sides facing and matching notches, machine-stitch the side seams together. Serge or zigzag-stitch to clean-finish the raw edges. Press the seams flat first, then to one side.

- -

Step 2   Serge or zigzag-stitch to clean-finish the raw edge of the hem. Press up a ⅜" (1 cm) hem allowance. From the right side of the skirt, topstitch the hem in place.

- -

Step 3   For the waist treatment on the Flirty Skirt, here's a technique from ready-to-wear. Measure your waist circumference. Cut a length of ¾" (2 cm)-wide knitted elastic so that it is 3" to 5" (7.5 to 12.5 cm) smaller than your own waist measurement. For example, if the actual waist measurement is 38" (96.5 cm), as shown in the photograph, cut 35" (89 cm) of elastic. To make a tighter band, cut the elastic an extra 1" (2.5 cm) or 2" (5 cm) shorter.

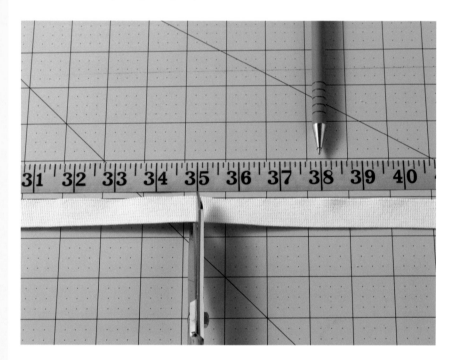

Step 4   Overlap the elastic ½" (1.3 cm), and secure with a pin.

Step 5   Machine-stitch the overlap by sewing a figure 8.

Step 6   Insert straight pins to divide the elastic into eight equal sections.

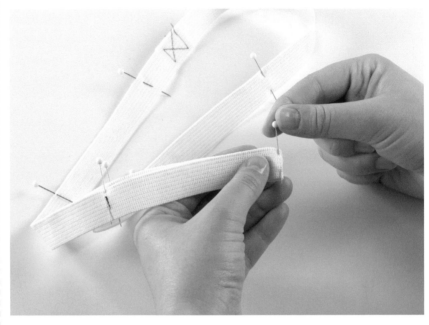

Step 7   Next, divide the skirt's waist into eight equal sections. Pin the elastic to the inside of the skirt waist, matching each of the eight sections.

The Zigzag Treatment

Following the instruction in your sewing machine manual, set your machine to a wide zigzag stitch. Following the raw edge of the skirt waist, zigzag the elastic to the inside waist edge. Stretch the elastic to fit each section as you sew. Pull each pin out as you approach it. Do not sew over the pins!

The Serger Treatment

A three- or four-thread serger will give a nice finish to the waist edge of your skirt. Serge around the edge of the elastic and skirt, stretching the elastic to fit each section and removing each pin as you approach it.

Step 8 To attach the elastic to the skirt, work with your serger, or select the zigzag stitch on your sewing machine. A serger produces a professional finish, but the zigzag stitch serves just as well.

Before you begin serging the waist, disengage the serger knife. This is a simple but important step, because if you nick the elastic even in the tiniest way, you'll shorten its life and you might find your waistline bagging out. How embarrassing to have your skirt slide down when least expected!

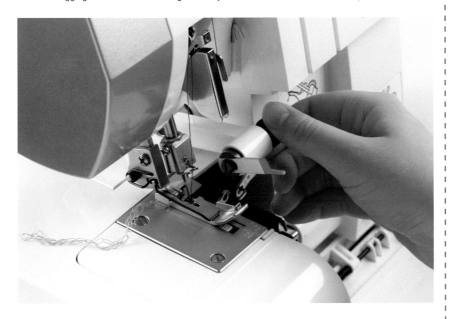

Step 9 Encase the elastic by folding it to the wrong side of the skirt. Place pins around the waistband to hold the elastic in place in equal sections.

Step 10 From the inside of the skirt, stitch along the lower edge. Use a long stitch and sew ⅛" to ¼" (3 to 6 mm) away from the serged or zigzagged edge. Stretch the band taut equally in front and back of the needle as you sew. Pull the pins out as you approach each one.

Step 11 When the stitching is complete, take the skirt to the ironing board, and steam the waist area by holding the iron over, but not touching, the fabric.

Step 12 Allow the skirt to sit until completely cool and dry. You will notice that the waistband shrank to form even gathers.

For cooler weather, the Flirty Skirt in a worsted wool, worn with matching blouse (page 62) and a flannel jacket (page 104)

For your spring wardrobe, the Flirty Skirt in a colorful print, worn with cotton blouse (page 62) and a corduroy jacket (page 104)

More Style Options

IF THE PATTERN FITS, keep wearing it! Here are two simple design variations that will help you create Flirty Skirt variations for your mix-and-match wardrobe.

Flirty Skirt with Sheer Overlay

For a feminine and romantic style, make the Flirty Skirt in two layers of fabric. Choose a satin for the underlayer and a sheer fabric like chiffon for the overlayer, and you'll have a very pretty skirt.

Cut the six skirt pieces in each fabric. Construct each skirt following the instructions on pages 56–59. Before applying the elastic to the waist, put the satin skirt (the underlayer) inside the sheer skirt (the overlayer).

Attach the skirts at the waist with two basting seams: the first 1½" (4 cm) away from the raw edge and the second ⅜" (1 cm) from the raw edge. Continue with the waistband instructions to finish your new skirt. Remove the basting stitches after you have completed the elastic waistband.

Bias-Cut Skirt

You can make a bias-cut skirt simply by cutting each piece of the pattern on the bias, or at a 45-degree angle to the selvage. However, most fabrics are not wide enough to allow you to place the angled pieces on a folded length of fabric. Instead, you must open your fabric so it's only a single layer and then cut each piece separately, six times, as shown on pages 54–55.

This little bit of extra work will pay off when you see the results. A skirt cut on the bias has a beautiful flow. In fact, you might also find it visually more slimming than a skirt cut on the straight grain. After you've cut out the skirt pieces, construct the skirt just as you normally would, following the instructions on pages 56–59.

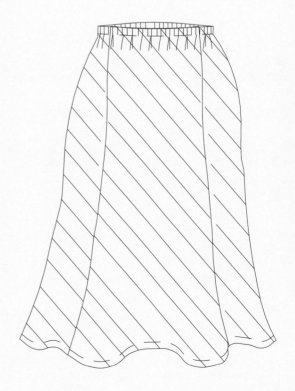

Shapely Blouse

THIS VERSATILE BLOUSE is a wonderful basic garment to have in your wardrobe—great with pants, skirts, jackets, and vests. Depending on your fabric choices, it is perfect for casual wear, business attire, and special occasions. The blouse has a flattering curved hemline and a button-front closure, but you could use snaps instead. The torso darts in the front and the back look very nice on women who have a defined waistline. If you have a straight or full waistline, leave the darts unstitched. For your neckline, the simplest variation is the faced neckline. Step up the styling with a rounded or pointed collar. Choose a cap sleeve for summer and a long sleeve for cooler weather. The long sleeve is made in two pieces so that you can easily fine-tune the fit for your arms.

Shapely Blouse in a cotton blend, worn with a rayon batik skirt (page 52)

Shapely Blouse in cotton blend, worn with cordoroy pants (page 84)

Shapely Blouse in a cotton blend, worn with pants in poly crepe (page 84)

Suggested Fabric Layout for All Sizes

Here are the suggested fabric layouts for your pattern pieces to make the most efficient use of the fabric and position the pieces as needed on the fabric grain. Please note the suggested width of the fabric, and also whether the fabric is folded or single ply.

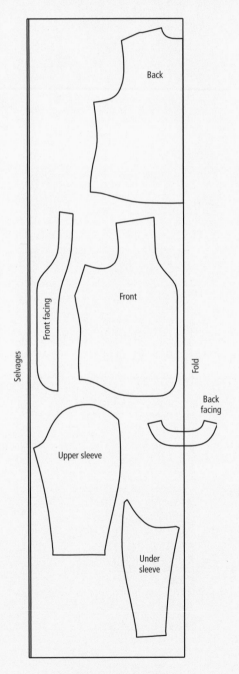

Faced neckline with long sleeve
Fabric width: 45" to 60" (115 to 150 cm)

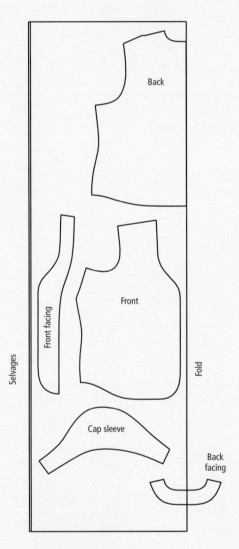

Faced neckline with cap sleeve
Fabric width: 45" to 60" (115 to 150 cm)

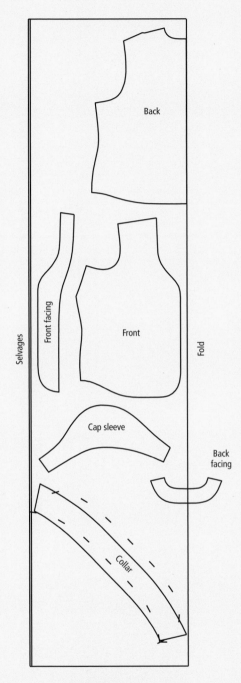

Collar with cap sleeve
Fabric width: 45" to 60" (115 to 150 cm)

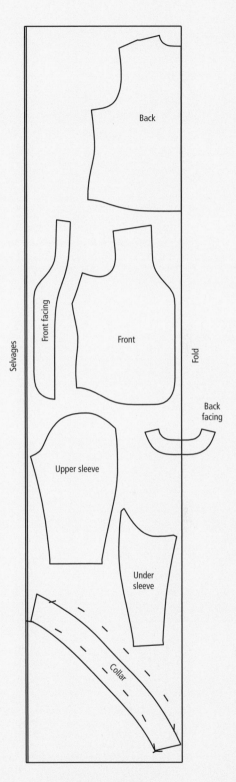

Long sleeve with collar
Fabric width: 45" to 60" (115 to 150 cm)

Custom Fitting

Compare your own measurements to the Body Measurement Chart (page 33) and review the Finished Garment Measurements Chart (page 135). Make a note of any necessary adjustments.

It's always a good idea to make a quick-fit muslin when making a new pattern (page 39). When you've made the muslin, evaluate the fit. If you think the Shapely Blouse pattern needs tweaking to fit your unique shape, follow the helpful advice in The Perfect Fit Guide chapter (pages 38–51).

Fabrics and Notions

Refer to the layouts on pages 64–65 the fabric requirements on page 135. For the best results, choose a woven fabric that is light to medium weight with a fluid drape. Make sure that the fabric feels good to you and flatters your body. I have made this blouse in silk, cotton, polyester, rayon, wool, and synthetic blends.

Cap sleeve, without collar

Long sleeve, without collar

Long sleeve, with pointed collar

Long sleeve, with rounded collar

Step 1   Interface the front and back facings. If you are choosing to make a blouse with a collar, also interface one piece of the collar of your choice, as indicated on the pattern.

Step 2   Sew the darts on the front and back. Press the darts toward the center. On the front, press the bust darts down.

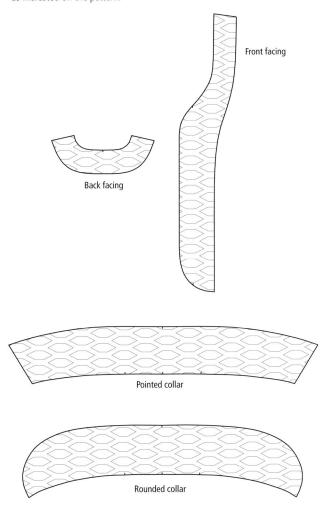

Front facing

Back facing

Pointed collar

Rounded collar

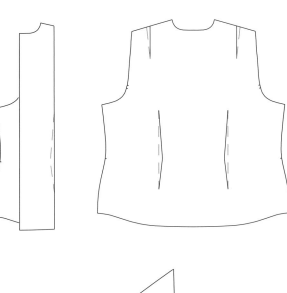

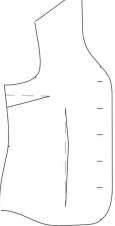

Step 3   With right sides together, sew the front to the back and the front facing to back facing along the shoulder seams.

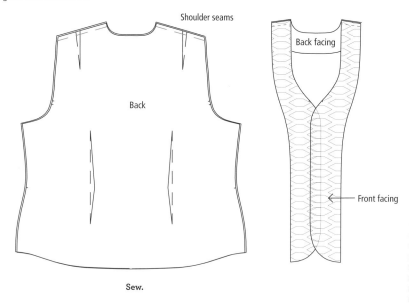

Sew.

Step 4   Sew the side seams together.

Step 5   Serge the raw edges of the shoulder seams and the side seams closed. Press the seams toward the back.

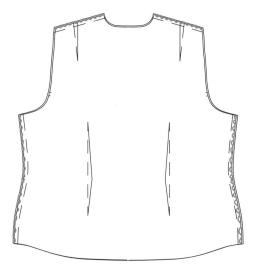

Serge.

Step 6   Serge the raw edges on the outside of the facings.

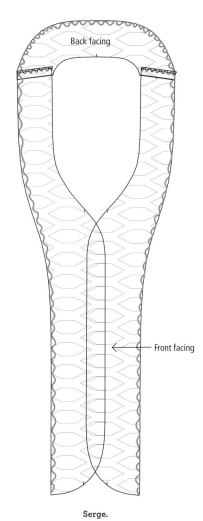

Serge.

Continue with the instructions to add a collar if you choose to make one. If you are not making a collar, go to step 12, and continue with the instructions for the facing. (If you'd like to add piping to your blouse, now's the time to do it. See pages 74–79.)

Step 7   If you are adding a collar, choose either the pointed or the rounded collar. With right sides facing, stitch the upper and under collars together, leaving the neckline edge open.

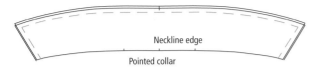

Neckline edge

Pointed collar

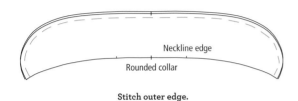

Neckline edge

Rounded collar

Stitch outer edge.

Step 8   Turn the collar to its finished position and press.

Step 9   To finish the collar, edgestitch from the top side around the outside edge.

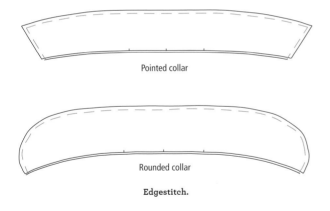

Pointed collar

Rounded collar

Edgestitch.

Step 10   With right sides together, pin the finished collar to the right side of the blouse. Match the collar notches to the CB notch and the shoulder seams. Match the finished ends of the collar to the CF notches on the blouse neckline.

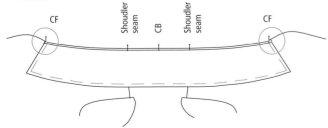

CF   Shoudler seam   CB   Shoudler seam   CF

Step 11   Machine-baste collar to the neckline edge from the CF notch to the CF notch.

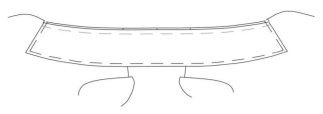

Machine-baste along the neck edge.

Step 12   With right sides together, pin the facing to the blouse, matching the notches at the CB, the shoulders, and the CF. (If you are making a collar, sandwich it between the facing and the blouse.)

Step 13   Stitch the facing to the blouse, from the hem edge up the CF, along the neckline, and then down to the other hem edge. Remove the pins as you sew.

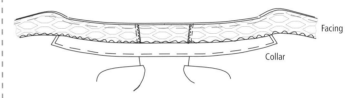

Facing

Collar

Step 14   Turn the facing to its finished position and press. (You will topstitch this area later, after you've completed the hem.)

Step 15   The hem is often sewn last, but I like to sew it now because there are fewer blouse pieces to get in the way and become wrinkled. Serge the raw edges of the hem. Press up 3⁄8" (1 cm). Stitch the hem in place either by hand or by machine.

The Shapely Blouse in rayon batik complements the color, fabric, and style of these rayon-blend capri pants.

Step 16 On the right side, topstitch, starting where the hemstitching ends. Continue around the outside edge of the front around the neckline and back down to the hemstitching. If your blouse has a collar, stop topstitching at the CF point, where the collar is inserted. Then resume topstitching on the other side, from the the CF point to the hem.

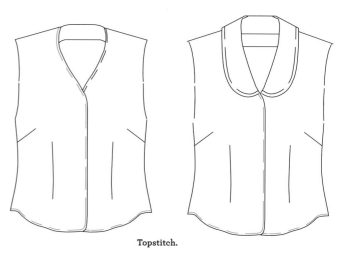

Topstitch.

Step 17 For the CF closures, apply snaps, or stitch buttonholes and sew on buttons. Continue with the instructions for cap sleeves or long sleeves, depending on which you choose.

STEPS FOR CAP SLEEVES

Step 1   Serge the raw edge of the hem. Prepare the hem by pressing up ⅜" (1 cm) along the lower edge.

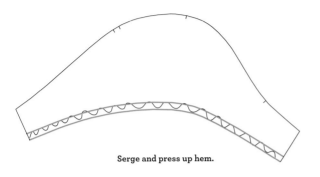

Serge and press up hem.

Step 2   With right sides together, sew the underarm seams. Serge the raw edges of the seams together. Press the underarm seam toward the back sleeve.

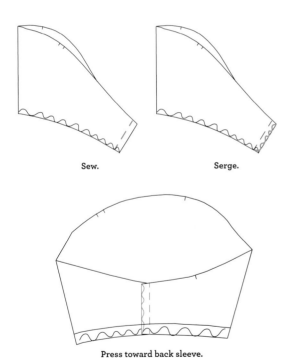

Sew.   **Serge.**

Press toward back sleeve.

Step 3   Stitch the sleeve hem either by hand or by machine.

Step 4   Machine-baste a row of stitching along the sleeve cap just inside the seam allowance, from the front sleeve notch, past the shoulder notch, and then to the back sleeve notch. Pull the basting threads gently to gather lightly. With the right side up, drape the sleeve cap over a tailor's ham. With your steam iron, shrink the fabric slightly to remove as much of the puckering as possible. Aim to make the sleeve cap rounded and smooth.

Basting stitches for easing

Step 5   Pin the sleeve into the armscye with right sides together, matching notches and underarm seams. Stitch in place, removing pins as you sew. Remove the basting threads. Serge the raw edges of the armhole.

Often, to secure threads at the beginning and end of a seam, you backstitch—but backstitches can look untidy in topstitching. A neat alternative is lockstitching. Change your needle stitch length to zero, and sew three or four times in the same position at the beginning and at the end of your seam.

The long-sleeve blouse works beautifully with either the pointed- or rounded-style collar—and depending on the fabric—is just as suited to warm weather as to cool.

STEPS FOR LONG SLEEVES

Step 1 With right sides together and matching double notches, sew the upper sleeve to the under sleeve along the back sleeve seam. Serge the raw edges of the back sleeve seam. Press the seam toward the under sleeve.

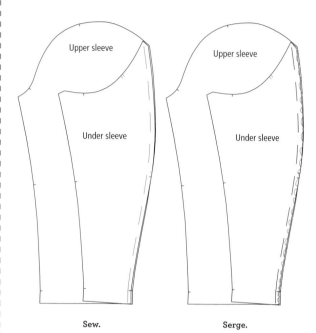

Sew.   Serge.

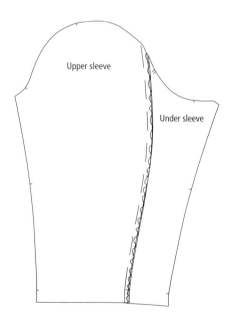

Press toward under sleeve.

Hem Like a Pro

A little preparation makes for a neater hem later. Serge the raw edge of the hem. Use the notches as your guide and press up a 1" (2.5 cm) hem.

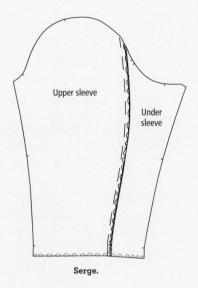

Upper sleeve

Under sleeve

Serge.

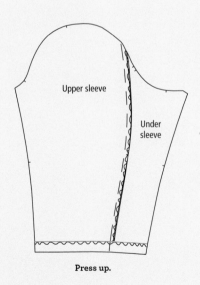

Upper sleeve

Under sleeve

Press up.

Step 2   With right sides together, sew the underarm seams. Serge the raw edges of the seam.

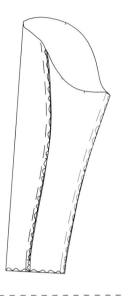

Step 3   Press the seam toward the upper sleeve.

Step 4   Fold the pressed hem up into its finished position. Stitch the sleeve hem by hand, or topstitch by machine.

Step 5   Machine-baste along the sleeve cap just inside the seam allowance, from the front sleeve seam, over the cap, past the shoulder notch, and to the back sleeve seam.

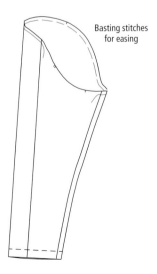

Basting stitches for easing

Step 6   Pull the basting threads gently to gather lightly. With the right side up, drape the sleeve cap over a tailor's ham. With your steam iron, shrink out as much of the puckering as possible. Aim to make the sleeve cap rounded and smooth.

Step 7   Pin the sleeve into the armscye with right sides facing. Match the notches as follows:

- Shoulder notch at the top of the cap to the shoulder seam
- Back sleeve notch to the double notch on the back armhole
- Side seam notch to the blouse side seam
- Front sleeve notch to the front sleeve notch

Step 8   Stitch the sleeve in place, removing pins as you sew. Remove the basting stitches. Serge the raw edges of the armhole.

More Style Options

IF THE PATTERN FITS, keep wearing it! Here are some simple design ideas and pattern-making steps that will help you create stylish details on the Shapely Blouse—and add even more variety to your mix-and-match wardrobe.

A little bit of piping adds interest to the edging of a simple blouse.

Piping

Give your simple blouse an upscale twist! You will need only about ½ yd. (0.5 m) of fabric. I love to combine coordinating plaids. You can also create piping in a contrasting or matching color. Complete the construction of the blouse up to the point where you'll add the facing. Apply the piping first, and then continue with the facing.

I like to use cotton cording for piping because it is soft and easy to handle. One problem with cotton cording, however, is that it's susceptible to shrinkage and it may appear puckered. Avoid disaster by preshrinking. A quick way to preshrink the cording is to hold a steam iron on top and apply steam in several good bursts. Don't touch the cording with the iron—let the steam do the work. Allow the cording to cool and dry before handling.

Step 1   Prepare the piping filler—also called cording. There are many kinds of piping filler, but I prefer cotton about ¼" (6 mm) in diameter. You will need about 2½ yd. (2.5 m) of cording for this blouse.

Step 2   To create the piping, cover the cording with fabric that has been cut on the bias so it is flexible and will bend smoothly around curves. To cut bias strips of fabric, follow the instructions on pages 78–79.

Step 3   Begin pinning the piping at the CB of the blouse. Fold the piping in half lengthwise, and place the halfway point at the CB notch along the neckline. Place your work flat on the table. Pin the piping onto the right side of the blouse, raw edge to raw edge. (Be careful not to let the piping hang off the edge of the table. Bias-cut fabric can stretch easily, which will cause distortion and rippling.)

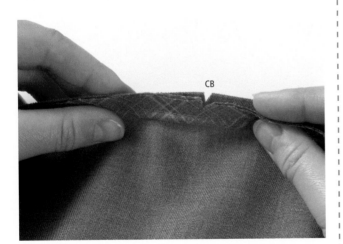

Step 4   Begin sewing at the lower curve of the blouse. Leave a 2" (5 cm) tail free.

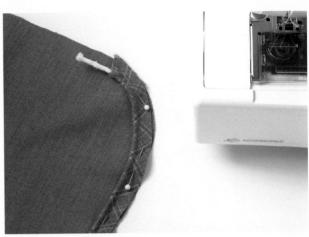

> **Many new sewing machines** have specialty feet designed for piping applications. Refer to your sewing machine manual. You may discover that a funny-looking attachment is your new best friend!

Step 5   Insert your needle about 1" (2.5 cm) away from the CF notch along the hemline. Sew slowly and evenly, being careful to remove pins as you approach the presser foot. Keep the raw edges even to the edge of the blouse and keep the foot snug against the filler.

Step 6 Finish stitching 1" (2.5 cm) away from the CF notch along the hemline. Leave a 2" (5 cm) tail unsewn on the piping.

Step 7 Place the facing with its right side against the piping. Match up the notches for the CB, shoulder seams, and the CF.

Step 8 Insert the pins on the blouse side, within the seam allowance.

Step 9 Place the garment on the sewing machine with the facing against the machine bed. This way, you can see your previous stitching, stay on the same path, and avoid stitching into the cording.

Step 10 Before inserting your needle, pull the piping tail away from the garment. Using a ⅜" (1 cm) seam allowance, begin sewing at the lower edge of the facing. Backstitch to firmly secure the facing to the blouse as you begin. Carefully merge your sewing onto the stitching line from the previous step as you sew over the little bump of the piping. Follow the path of your previous stitching exactly.

Step 11 When you've completed your sewing, trim off the piping tail.

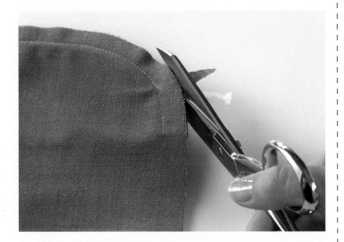

Step 12 Turn the facing to its finished position.

Step 13 Press the piped area on the inside and outside of the blouse, being careful to open the seams without flattening the piping. Continue constructing the rest of your blouse, as described on pages 67–71.

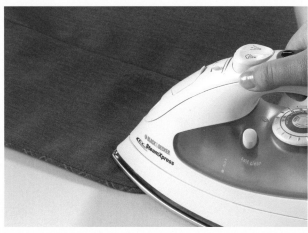

Easy, Accurate Piping

To cut bias strips of your fabric, lay a ruler across the fabric on a 45-degree angle to the straight of grain. To calculate how wide the strip should be, wrap your fabric around the cording, pin, and then add seam allowances for the flange. (The flange is the part of the piping that will be anchored or sandwiched between the blouse and the facing.) For this blouse, a nice width for the cover is 1¼" (3 cm). This width will be adequate to cover the cording and also to leave a flange a tiny bit wider than the ⅜" (1 cm) seam allowance.

Chalk along your ruler to create even strips that are 1¼" (3 cm) wide.

Cut along the chalk line. You will need about 2½ yd. (2.5 m) of bias strips for this blouse. It's difficult to cut this much bias strip in one length, so you'll have to join your strips.

JOINING STRIPS

You must join the ends of the strips on the straight grain. Place the ends right sides together, centering so that you have a little pointy part extending at each side. Sew with a narrow seam allowance. Press the seam joints open.

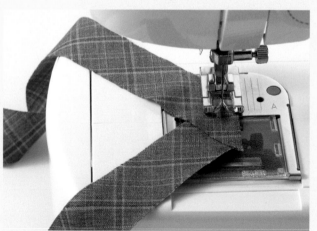

Next, to avoid unsightly ripples in your bias strip, fold the strip lengthwise evenly, without pulling. Press the strip a little at a time, being careful not to stretch the strip. A slight crease will form at the fold. This crease will help you insert the cording accurately. When the insertion is complete, you'll steam out the crease.

Sew slowly. No need to use pins—instead, use the center crease as your guide for accuracy. Push the cording toward the crease with your fingers and keep the raw edges of the bias strip even.

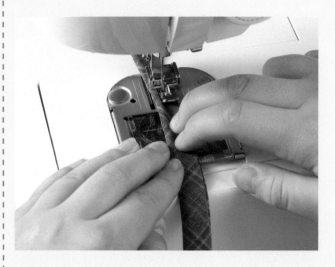

When you come to the end of the strip, clip the excess cord, leaving a tail of cording that extends about 1" (2.5 cm). Gently steam the crease out of the piping.

INSERTING THE FILLER

Sandwich the cording inside the bias strip, pushing it up to the center crease of the bias strip. Leave a tail of about 1" (2.5 cm) of cord extending out of the bias strip. When you sew the piping, keep your stitches snug up to the cording. I like to use a zipper foot for better control.

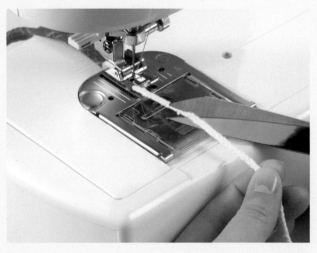

Fast Cuff

Instead of hemming your long sleeve, apply this fast cuff and quickly give your blouse a classic, tailored-shirt look. With this quick pattern-drafting technique, you can easily add cuffs to any of your blouse patterns.

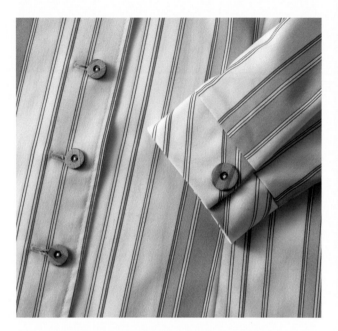

This long-sleeved blouse has gentle stripes, a pointed collar, and a fast cuff on the sleeves—all of which contribute to the crisp, tailored look.

Step 1 With ruler, pencil, and sheet of paper, draw a line that measures the circumference of your sleeve along the wrist edge. Add ⅜" (1 cm) at each end for the seam allowance. Next, decide how deep you want your cuff to be. Draw another line to this measurement, perpendicular to your first line, adding ⅜" (1 cm) at each end.

A standard depth for a cuff is between 2" to 3" (5 to 7.5 cm). If you are not sure which depth will look good on you, consult your fingers! Measure the length of your little finger if you're making a short cuff or your middle finger for a longer cuff. Either length will be proportionate to your body.

Step 2 Fold your pattern paper along the wrist line. Cut out the cuff from this double layer of paper. Notch at the foldline.

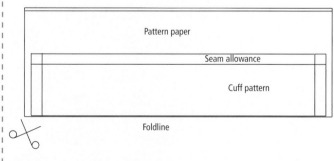

Step 3 Trace half the cuff to make an interfacing pattern. Label your pattern pieces: "Cuff (Cut 2 of fabric)" and "Interfacing (Cut 2)."

Step 4   Draw on a grainline that runs in the direction of the length of your arm. Include another that runs on the bias (45 degrees to the length line). You can cut the fabric in either direction. (You may want to cut striped fabric on the bias to create interesting patterning.)

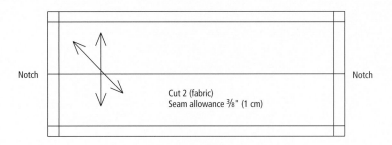

Notch

Cut 2 (fabric)
Seam allowance ⅜" (1 cm)

Notch

Cut 2 (interfacing)

Step 5   Cut out your fabric and interfacing pieces. (Choose a lightweight interfacing appropriate for your fabric.) Using the notches as a guide, fold the cuff into its finished position. Press a crease along the foldline. Fuse the interfacing to the wrong side of one half of the cuff, up to the crease.

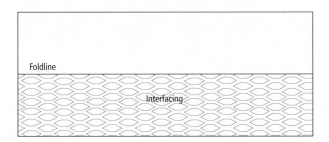

Foldline

Interfacing

Step 6   Fold the cuff right sides together along the side seam line. Stitch closed using a ⅜" (1 cm) seam allowance. Press the seam open. (This seam will be completely enclosed, so you don't need to serge or otherwise clean-finish the raw edges.)

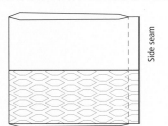

Side seam

Step 7   Turn the cuff right side out. With right sides facing, pin the raw edges of the folded cuff to the sleeve along the wrist edge. Position the cuff seam on the underarm section of the sleeve, halfway between the front and back sleeve seams. Stitch the cuff to the sleeve using a ⅜" (1 cm) seam allowance. Serge to finish the raw edges.

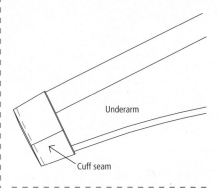

Underarm

Cuff seam

Step 8   Press the seam upward to the inside of the sleeve. Press the cuff down into its finished position.

Step 9   You could also dress up the cuff with buttons. Put on the sleeve, and, at your wrist bone, pinch in a fold. (Make sure that you have enough room to slide the cuff off your hand.) Mark the fold. Then secure the fold in place with one or two buttons—your choice.

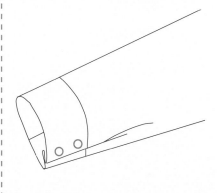

Button Treatments

Change the buttons, change the look. Turn an everyday piece you might wear to the office into a new addition to your evening wardrobe. Buttons can be subtle, **functional items** or bold, **decorative accessories**. Experiment to see which styles you like best. As quick as you can sew on a button, you can change the style of a simple blouse. Have fun at the button counter, and buy more than one type of button so you can experiment.

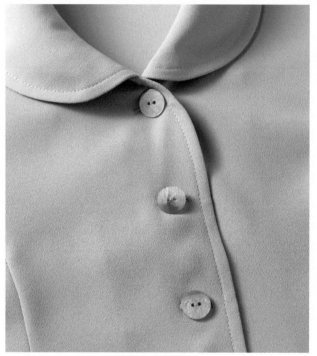

Shell buttons

Decorative pearl buttons

Covered buttons are among my favorite treatments—and you can make them yourself. There are many kits on the market that will make the job of covering buttons very simple and give you a professional finish.

Here we use a kit with ⅞" (2 cm) buttons. The button kit comes with a flexible button form, a hard plastic plunger, and two-piece button blanks. The two-piece blanks are usually metal and are designed to fit together back to front with fabric wrapped and sandwiched in between.

Covered button kit

Step 1 Cut a strip of fabric on the bias for the buttons. If your material is delicate, you can apply a lightweight fusible interfacing to the wrong side of the fabric. Cut a circle of your fabric about ⅜" (1 cm) larger than the button form.

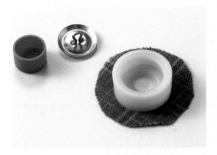

Step 2 Use the fabric circle as a pattern for cutting the remaining circles. Cut one circle for each button.

Step 3 Place the front of a button blank onto the wrong side of one of your fabric circles. Place the fabric circle and the front of the button blank evenly and snugly into the form.

Step 4 With your fingers, push all the fabric to the inside of the button.

Step 5 Place the button backing into the button form, making sure to sandwich all the fabric neatly.

Step 6 Place the plunger, open side down, onto the button back. Notice how the plunger fits exactly inside the rim of the button back.

Step 7 With both thumbs, press hard on the plunger to lock the button back and the fabric into the button front.

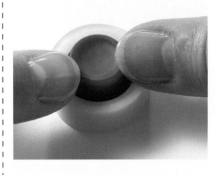

Step 8 Press the back of the form to pop your new covered button out. A new button is born! Repeat these steps until all your buttons are covered.

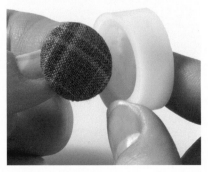

Classic Fly-Front Pants

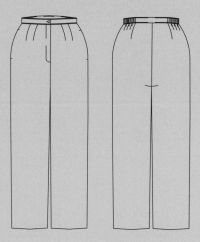

THIS CLASSIC PAIR of pants will be your wardrobe's best friend day and night. You can make this versatile garment in many fabrics to take you through casual everyday, business, and evening events.

These pants have straight legs, front and back no-pouch darts, no-gape inseam pockets, and a fly-front zipper closure. For comfort and flexible fit, the waistband includes side-back elastic—so discreet that you can wear your blouse tucked in if you want. This garment provides a comfortable solution to those puffy days. It is designed to drape smoothly past any lumps, bumps, and fitting challenges and will accommodate a tummy and high padding below the waistline. There is also plenty of room for a full seat and hip.

Classic Fly-Front Pants in corduroy, worn with cotton blouse (page 62) and matching jacket (page 104)

The capri pants variation, in worsted wool, lined and worn with worsted wool plaid blouse (page 62)

Classic Fly-Front Pants in poly crepe, worn with a cotton blouse (page 62)

Custom Fitting

Compare your own measurements to the Body Measurement Chart (page 33) and review the Finished Garment Measurements Chart (page 136). Note any necessary adjustments.

It's a good idea to make a quick-fit muslin when making a new pattern, especially when making pants (page 39). When you've made the muslin, evaluate the fit. If you think the pants pattern needs tweaking, follow the advice in The Perfect Fit Guide chapter (pages 38–51).

Fabrics and Notions

Refer to the layout on page 88 and the fabric requirements on page 136 for the Classic Fly-Front Pants. For casual wear, make the pants in a light- to medium-weight corduroy. The corduroy for the sample shown on page 84 is a blend of cotton with 3 percent spandex. The spandex adds comfort and a smooth finish.

For office wear, consider making the pants in worsted wool for winter or in cool blends of microfiber and spandex for the warmer months. Worsted wool is a natural fabric that breathes and resists wrinkles. For soft career dressing, also consider rayon or smooth cottons. For evening, the classic pants look elegant in a silk or polyester crepe. If making the pants in wool or in a delicate fabric, you could line them. Or you could vary the style by shortening them into cropped or capri pants. In this chapter, you'll learn how to do it all.

Suggested Fabric Layout for All Sizes

The suggested fabric layout for your pattern pieces (page 88) will help you make the most efficient use of the fabric and position the pieces as needed on the fabric grain. Please note the suggested width of the fabric, and also whether the fabric is folded or single ply.

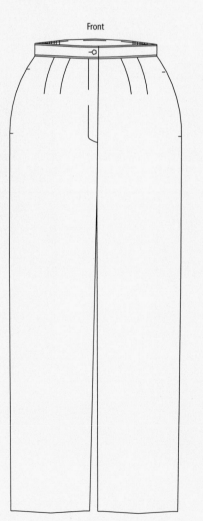

Front

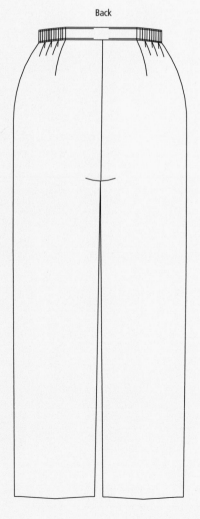

Back

Step 1   Apply lightweight, fusible interfacing according to the manufacturer's instructions to the wrong sides of the:

- Front-fly extension opening
- Waistband, excluding elastic casing pocket opening
- Front side seam at pocket opening
- Front pocket bag

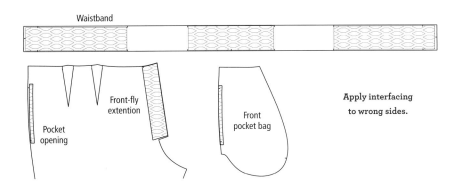

Waistband

Pocket opening

Front-fly extention

Front pocket bag

Apply interfacing to wrong sides.

Step 2   On the front and back pieces, with right sides facing and matching notches, fold each dart along its center. Sew from the waist edge to the point.

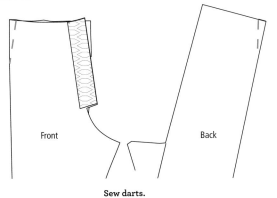

Front

Back

Sew darts.

Step 3   Press darts toward the center of the garment.

Step 4   At the pocket notches on the front and back pants pieces and on all pocket bag pieces, sew a reinforcing stitch ⅜" (1 cm) from the raw edge.

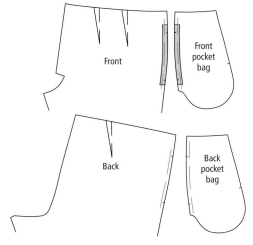

Front

Front pocket bag

Back

Back pocket bag

Reinforce opening with stitching.

Step 5   With right sides together and matching notches, pin the front pocket bag to the pant front, and the back pocket to the pant back. Stitch along the pocket opening with a ⅜" (1 cm) seam allowance. Stitch between the notches only. Backstitch at the beginning and end of the seam.

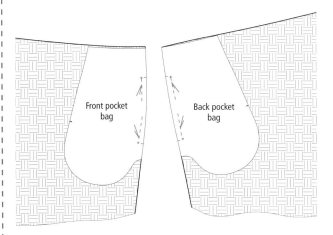

Front pocket bag

Back pocket bag

Stitch between notches.

Step 6   Clip the pocket notches on the **front** pocket bag and pants **front** only, all the way to the reinforcing stitches.

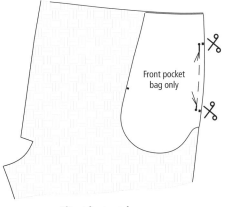

Front pocket bag only

Clip at front notches.

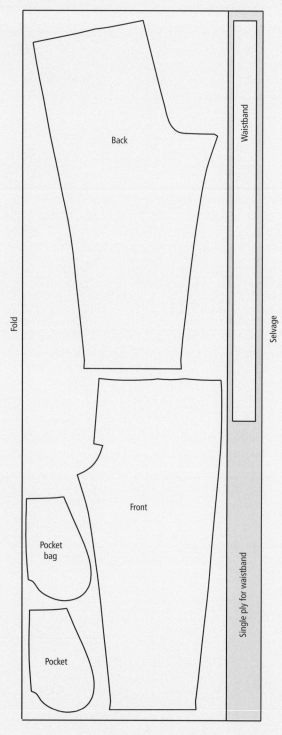

Fabric width: 54" to 60" (140 to 150 cm)

Step 7 On the pants front, press the seam allowance toward the pocket bag. Then, understitch the seam allowances to the pocket bag, starting and stopping ⅜" (1 cm) from each notch. **Do not understitch all the way up to the notch or it will be more difficult to complete the remaining construction.**

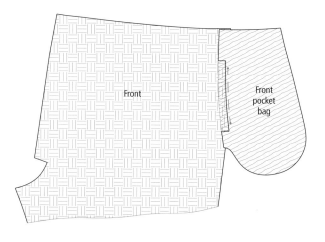

Step 8 Matching the raw edges and notches, and with the right sides together, pin the front and back pocket bags together. Sew around the **outside of the bag only.**

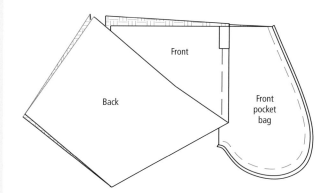

Step 9   Serge or zigzag-stitch to finish the raw edges of the pocket bags.

- -

Step 10   With the pants front and pants back right sides together, place the completed pocket unit against the wrong side of the pants front. Adjust the clipped upper and lower sections of the pocket and pant until they sandwich neatly between the pocket fabric and the pants back. Make sure that all raw edges meet evenly.

- -

Step 11   Pin the pieces to secure, and then machine-stitch from the waist edge to the upper pocket notch. Backstitch.

Step 12   Begin again at lower pocket notch with a backstitch and continue sewing along the side seam to the hem edge.

- -

Step 13   Machine-baste the upper edge of the pocket bag to the front pants ¼" (6 mm) from the raw edge.

- -

Step 14   Serge or zigzag-stitch the raw edges of the side seams together from waist edge to the hem, being careful to stay well clear of the straight stitching in the pocket area. Press seams flat first, and then press toward the back.

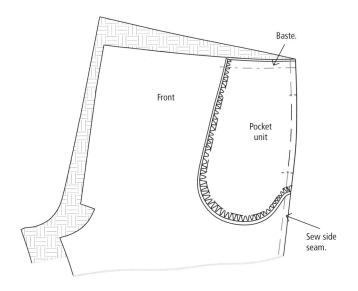

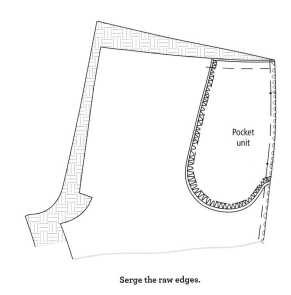

Serge the raw edges.

Hem Like a Pro

It might seem early, but the best time to press up the hem is the time when the legs are open and flat. Serge or zigzag-stitch the raw edge of the hem. Press up the hem, working with the notches as a guide. Then open up the hem. When you stitch the hem later, you won't have to spend a lot of time measuring and pinning. The hem is already creased and ready to go!

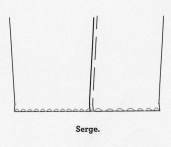

Serge.

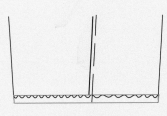

Press up hem.

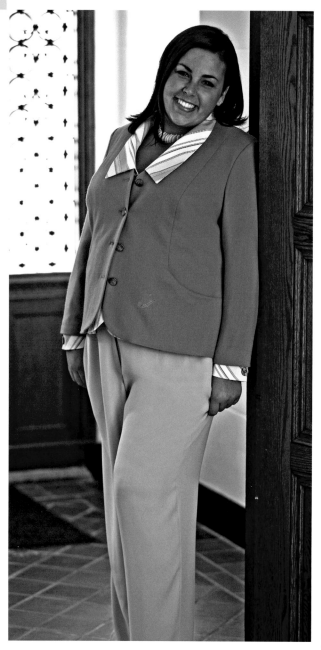

The Classic Fly-Front Pants in poly crepe, worn with cotton blouse (page 62) and wool flannel jacket (page 104)

Step 15   The pattern includes a fly-front zipper guide to help you achieve straight topstitching. Serge or zigzag-stitch the raw edges of the fly extensions and the front and back crotch.

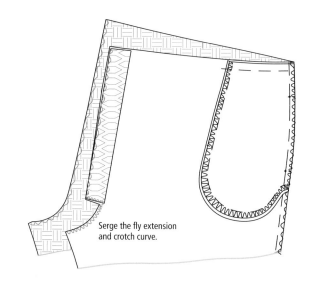

Serge the fly extension and crotch curve.

Step 16   With right sides facing, machine-baste the fly extensions together from the dot to the CF notch at the waist edge.

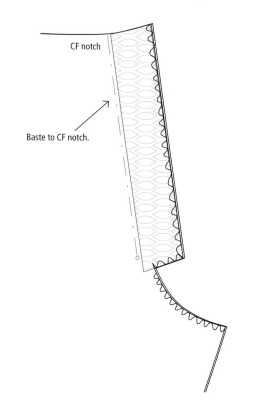

CF notch

Baste to CF notch.

Step 17   Working with a shorter stitch length, sew the fronts together at the crotch, beginning about 2" (5 cm) from the inside leg and stitching to the dot. To reinforce the stitching, stretch as you sew.

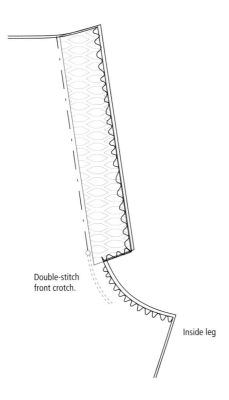

Double-stitch front crotch.

Inside leg

Step 18   Fold the right fly to the wrong side along the guideline. Press in place. Remove the basting stitches.

Have you ever had a seam break right under your zipper? It's almost impossible to fix! Here's how to protect yourself from future problems. Double-stitch the crotch curve below the fly, following the first set of stitching. Stretch as you sew, as this will build strength into the seam.

Step 19   Fold the serged edge of the left fly ⅜" (1 cm) to the left of the center front notch. Press in place. What you will end up with is a fold-back of 1" (2.5 cm) on the left fly and a fold-back of 1⅜" (3.5 cm) on the right fly.

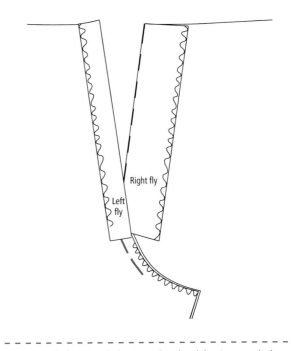

Right fly

Left fly

Step 20   **Left front:** With the zipper closed and the zipper teeth close to the pressed edge of the fly extension, position the metal stop even with the dot at the bottom of the fly opening. (You can conceal or trim any excess at the waistline edge when you've completed the fly construction.) With a zipper foot, edgestitch next to the zipper teeth through all thicknesses. Begin at the metal stop, and finish at the waist edge.

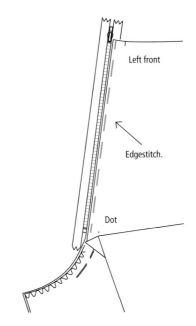

Left front

Edgestitch.

Dot

Step 21   Right front: Lap the right front over the left front, matching the guidelines at the center front. From the inside of the pants, extend the right fly extension, and position the unstitched side of the zipper face down. Stitching next to zipper teeth, sew through the zipper tape and **right fly extension only.**

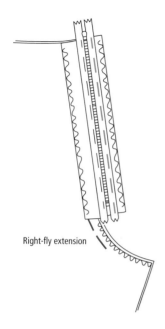

Right-fly extension

Step 22   Position the zipper so that the right fly extension is flat against the right front. From the right side of the pants, position the topstitch guide along the front fly crease. Mark along the guide with chalk, invisible marking pen, or basting stitches.

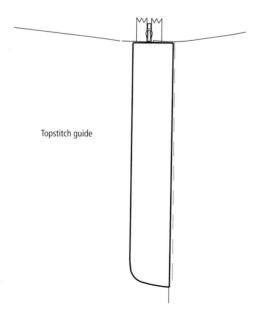

Topstitch guide

Step 23   From the bottom of the zipper, beginning with a backstitch, topstitch through all thicknesses, around the curve, and then straight up to the waist edge. Remove the guideline markings.

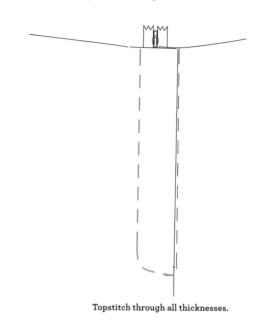

Topstitch through all thicknesses.

Step 24   With right sides together, match the raw edges and notches along the inseam. Sew the inside leg seam on each leg. Serge or zigzag-stitch to finish the raw seam edges. Press the seams flat and then to the back.

Step 25   Turn one leg right side out and the other right side in. Drop one leg inside the other so that they are right sides together. Matching inside seams, notches, and raw edges, pin the crotch seam.

Step 26   Stitch the crotch seams together, stretching through the curve as you sew. Double-stitch the back crotch curve for extra strength (page 91).

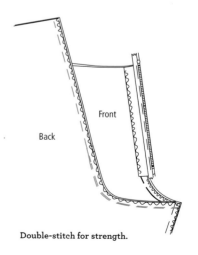

Front

Back

Double-stitch for strength.

Step 27   Serge or zigzag-stitch one length-wise edge of the waistband.

Wrong side

Step 28   Working with the notches as your guide, fold the band in half lengthwise, wrong sides together, and press.

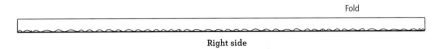

Fold

Right side

Step 29   Matching the notches at the CF, side seam, and the CB, pin the waistband to the right sides of the pants waist.

Step 30   Stitch in place, removing pins as you sew. Press the seam allowance up toward the band. If your zipper extends beyond the waistline edge, you may either trim off the excess length or lay the excess smoothly inside the surfaces of the waistband.

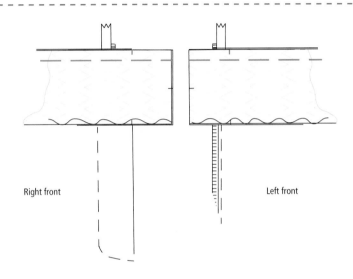

Right front

Left front

Step 31   Fold the waistband, right sides together, at the notch. Stitch the waistband together at each end, being careful to stay clear of the fabric on the fly front. On the right-hand side of the waistband, the stitching line should go straight up from the crease on the fly extension. On the left-hand side, the stitching follows a ⅜" (1 cm) seam allowance to provide a button extension.

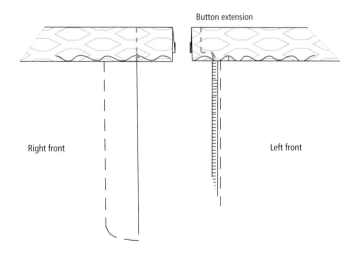

Button extension

Right front

Left front

Step 32 Refer to the elastic size chart and cut a length of elastic for your waist size.

Size	in	cm
14	7	18
16	7½	19
18	8	20.5
20	8½	21.5
22	9	23
24	9½	24

Step 33 Fold the elastic in half, and cut into two equal lengths. Position each length of elastic onto the casing section of the waistband against the fold line crease with ½" (1.3 cm) extending past the casing notch and onto the interfacing. Secure both ends of elastic by topstitching in place.

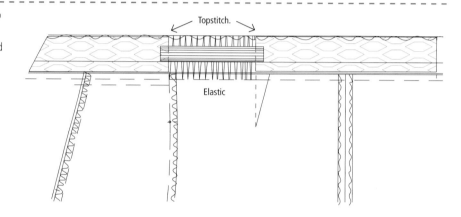

Step 34 Fold the waistband into its finished position, and pin along the casing. Topstitch at each end of the casing to help hold the elastic in place. While stretching the elastic taut, stitch a lengthwise seam through the center of the elastic. Backstitch at each end.

Step 35 Turn the remaining waistband into its finished position. From the right side of the pants, stitch in the ditch of the waistband seam (page 138). For greater control, use a zipper foot. Stretch the elastic section of the band, and remove the pins as you sew.

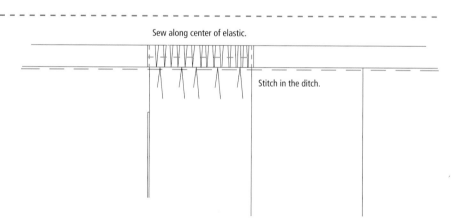

> **To return elastic to its original shape,** hold an iron above (not on) the waistband, and steam generously. Allow the garment to cool before handling.

Step 36   To add the closure, apply your choice of snaps, hook and eye, or button and buttonhole to the waistband at the CF.

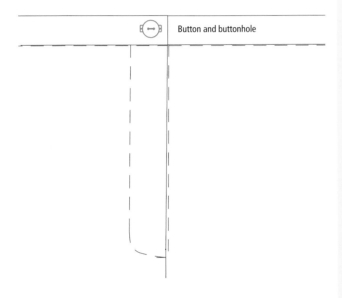

Button and buttonhole

Step 37   Machine- or hand-stitch a 1″ (2.5 cm) hem in place.

Add a Lining

A pants lining is a welcome addition if your fabric is delicate (like silk) or itchy (like many wools). In the fabric stores, you'll find lining fabrics made from rayon, polyester, silk, and cotton. Ask your fabric seller to recommend a suitable weight and fiber for your pants fabric.

Cut out the Front and Back leg pieces in lining. Follow the same construction steps as for the pant, omitting the steps for making the pocket and fly. At the CF notch, fold the lining to the wrong side and press a crease all the way to the zipper notch.

Complete the outer pant to the point of adding the waistband. Before applying the waistband, slide the lining into the pant with wrong side of lining facing the wrong side of the pant. Attach the lining to the pant waist edge with a long basting stitch inside the seam allowance. Continue with the steps for making the waistband. Hand-tack the lining to the zipper area.

More Style Options

IF THE PATTERN FITS, keep wearing it! Here are some simple design ideas and pattern-making steps that will help you create three pants variations for your mix-and-match wardrobe.

Capri Pants

Show off some leg! These great little pants offer all the comfort and flexibility of pants. You can wear them with high-heeled or flat shoes or boots. Change the fabric, and you can wear these pants to the beach or out on the town.

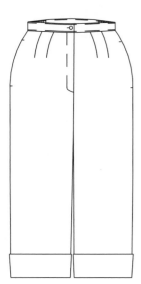 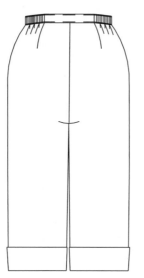

The capri pants variation, made in a rayon blend and worn with a rayon batik blouse (page 62)

The capri pants variation, made in worsted wool, lined and worn with a blouse in worsted wool plaid (page 62)

Step 1 Start with the classic pants pattern. Mark the legs to the length you want, or use the suggested line on the pattern. I'll show you two secrets to creating a pant cuff that you find only on expensive ready-to-wear. The width of the cuff is your choice.

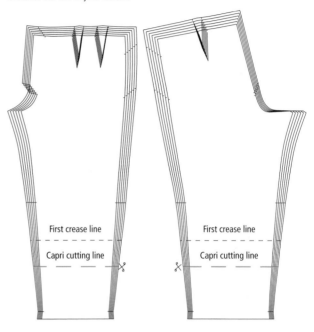

Step 2 Clip a little notch at the first crease line. You will use these notches as a guide to fold and press the cuff. To get a professional finish, press the creases in advance of the construction.

Step 3 With the wrong sides of the fabric facing up, press the first cuff fold.

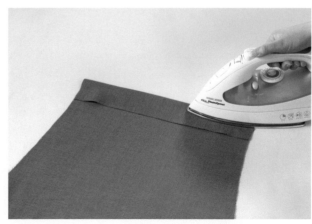

Step 4   Use the notches as your guide to fold the fabric.

Step 5   Using the first crease as your guide, fold the hem again toward the wrong side, and press a second crease.

The cuff on the capri pants is made with a double fold that is pressed well before serging or zigzag-stitching the raw edges and machine-stitching the finished hem.

Step 6   The cuff preparation is complete. Now, follow the pants sewing instructions on pages 87–95 until you reach the hem section. Serge or zigzag-stitch the raw edges of the cuffs.

Step 7   This next process is the second secret in the professional cuff construction. Turn up a hem that measures ⅜" (1 cm) beyond the first crease. Pin in place.

Step 8 Machine-stitch the hem in place. Notice how the crease wants to come up and hide the machine stitching, as you can see in the photo, below at right.

Step 9 Fold the cuff into its finished position.

Step 10 Secure the cuff by machine-sewing several stitches back and forth in the ditch of the side seam and the inseam.

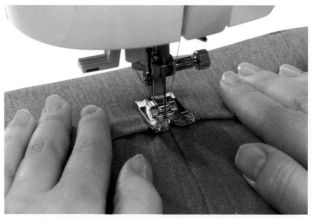

Step 11 Press the cuff from the inside.

Full Elastic Waist

A full elastic waist is a comfort feature. For many people, this is the only type of waistband to wear. If you always wear your tops *out* rather than tucked in, it makes sense to have the simple finish of a full elastic waist, rather than installing a zipper and tailored waistband.

Be careful when serging. If the elastic is nicked even the tiniest amount, it will quickly lose its elasticity. To avoid cutting into the elastic when serging, either remove or "rotate up" your serger knife.

Step 1   Lay the pattern pieces for the pants front and back on the fabric so that there is excess fabric along the waistline edge. Allow two times the height of your elastic for a simple folded-over "turn and serge" band. (I prefer 1¼" [3 cm]-wide sport-style elastic.)

- -

Step 2   Measure the width of your elastic. With tailor's chalk or a disappearing fabric marker, mark the height of a fold-over band along the waist edge of the front and back pants.

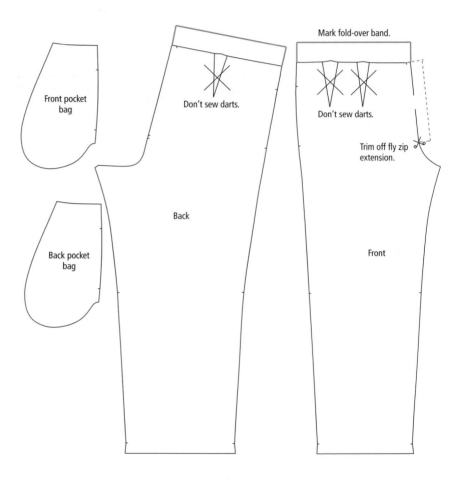

Step 3   Construct the pants according to the pattern instructions on pages 87–92, omitting the steps related to darts, fly, zipper, and separate waistband. When you reach the section on completing the waist, follow steps 4 through 7 below.

Step 4   Measure your waist (page 33). Cut one strip of 1¼" (3 cm)-wide sport-style elastic. I like to use sport-style elastic because it's easy to sew through and it retains its elasticity. Cut your elastic 3" to 5" (7.5 to 12.5 cm) less than your actual waist measurement. Overlap the ends, pin, and zigzag-stitch securely.

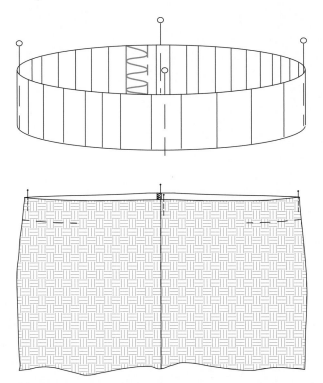

Step 5   Divide the elastic circle and the pants waist into equal quarters. Pin the elastic to the inside of the pants, matching quarter marks and the raw edges of the fabric.

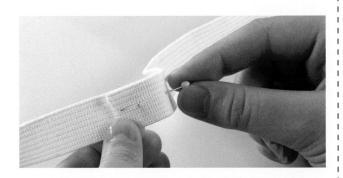

Step 6   With the elastic on top and the fabric below, serge or zigzag-stitch along the upper edge. As you sew, stretch the elastic evenly in front and behind the needle. Don't sew over the pins—pull them out as the needle approaches them. (Refer to the photos on pages 55–59 of the similar process of sewing the Flirty Skirt waistband.)

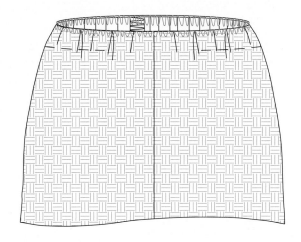

Step 7   Fold the elastic to the inside, and pin in place at the quarter marks. Topstitch two rows of stitching from the right side. Stretch the elastic evenly from behind and in front of the needle as you sew.

Step 8   Steam the elastic generously with your iron so that it recovers its original size. Allow to cool and dry before handling.

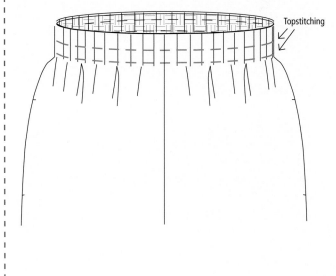

Topstitching

Belt Loops

The classic pants can be made with or without belt loops on the waistband. Belt loops are easy to add if you want to keep your style options open.

A belt is a wonderful accessory to give your ensemble a polished look. If you like wearing belts—or if you just want a sportier look—simply add belt loops to the pants waistband. The belt loops on this waistband will accommodate a belt that is up to 1" (2.5 cm) wide.

To give yourself a longer body line, wear a belt that is the same color as your blouse and pants. A contrasting color will draw attention to your waist and silhouette—you might like this effect or not. A decorative belt buckle worn under an open jacket also creates a slimming line.

Even if you don't always choose to wear a belt, adding belt loops to the classic pants gives you another style option.

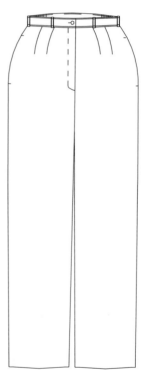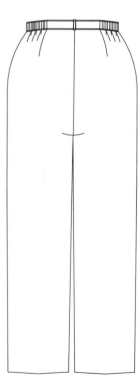

Step 1   Cut a strip of fabric that measures 15″ long by 1½″ (38 x 4 cm) wide. Along one length of the belt loop, serge or zigzag-stitch the raw edge.

Step 8   Position the belt loops onto the waistband at the CB, at the side seams, and halfway between the side seam and the CF.

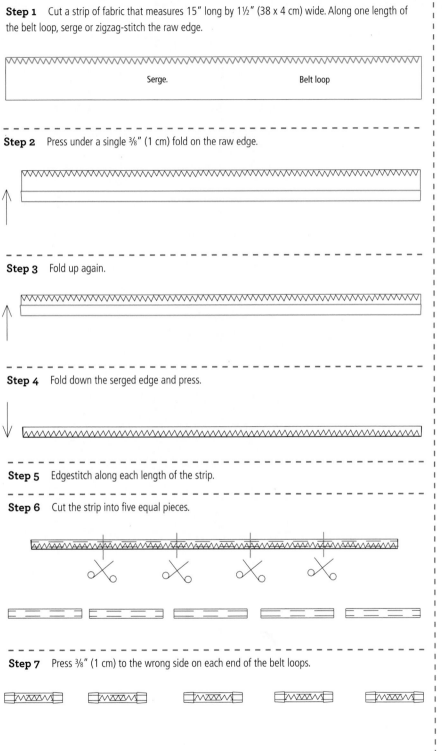

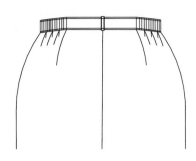

Step 2   Press under a single ⅜″ (1 cm) fold on the raw edge.

Step 3   Fold up again.

Step 4   Fold down the serged edge and press.

Step 9   Stitch in place.

Step 5   Edgestitch along each length of the strip.

Step 6   Cut the strip into five equal pieces.

Step 7   Press ⅜″ (1 cm) to the wrong side on each end of the belt loops.

Simple Slimming Jacket

THIS JACKET IS the all-important "third piece." Whenever you add a jacket to any two-piece outfit, you step up the styling. The princess seams, which originate at the shoulder and flow vertically over the body, are slimming and make for easy fit adjustments. From shoulders to bust, to waist, and over the hip—look at all the seams you can nip in or let out. Your jacket will fit like a glove!

This softly shaped garment can be lined or unlined. For closures, add traditional buttons, snaps, a dramatic brooch—or keep it simple and add nothing at all. The jacket's two-piece sleeves are smooth and easy-to-custom fit. Pockets are hidden within the curved hip seam. To frame your face, choose a simple faced neckline or add your choice of a pointed or rounded collar.

A lightweight, unlined version of the Simple Slimming Jacket in a rayon batik, worn with matching skirt (page 52) and cotton-blend blouse (page 62)

For special occasions, the Simple Slimming Jacket in metallic silver fabric, lined and worn with poly crepe blouse (page 62) with decorative buttons and poly crepe pants (page 84)

Simple Slimming Jacket in wool flannel, lined and worn with a cotton blend blouse (page 62) and poly crepe pants (page 84)

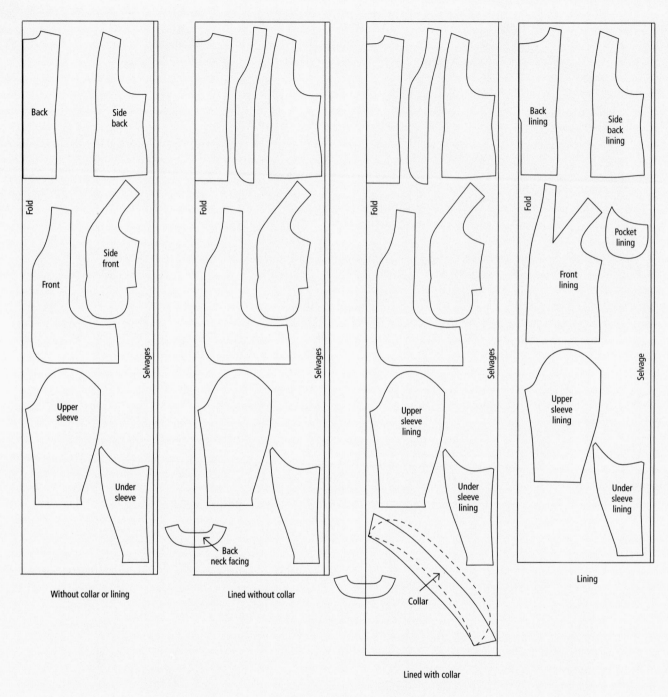

Back

Side
back

Fold

Front

Side
front

Selvages

Upper
sleeve

Under
sleeve

Without collar or lining

Fold

Selvages

Back
neck facing

Lined without collar

Fold

Selvages

Upper
sleeve
lining

Under
sleeve
lining

Collar

Lined with collar

Back
lining

Side
back
lining

Fold

Pocket
lining

Front
lining

Selvage

Upper
sleeve
lining

Under
sleeve
lining

Lining

Fabric width: 45" to 60" (115 to 150 cm)

Suggested Fabric Layout for All Sizes

At left are the suggested fabric layouts for your pattern pieces to make the most efficient use of the fabric and position the pieces as needed on the fabric grain. Please note the suggested width of the fabric, and also whether the fabric is folded or single ply.

Custom Fitting

Compare your own measurements to the Body Measurement Chart (page 33) and review the Finished Garment Measurements Chart (page 137). Make a note of any necessary adjustments.

It's always a good idea to make a quick-fit muslin when making a new pattern (page 39). When you've made the muslin, evaluate the fit. If you think the jacket pattern needs tweaking, follow the helpful advice in The Perfect Fit Guide chapter (pages 38–51).

Fabric and Notions

Refer to the layouts on the facing page and the fabric requirements on page 137 for the Simple Slimming Jacket. Choose woven or knit fabrics, such as wool flannel, crepe, gabardine, Ultrasuede, silk, linen, and rayon.

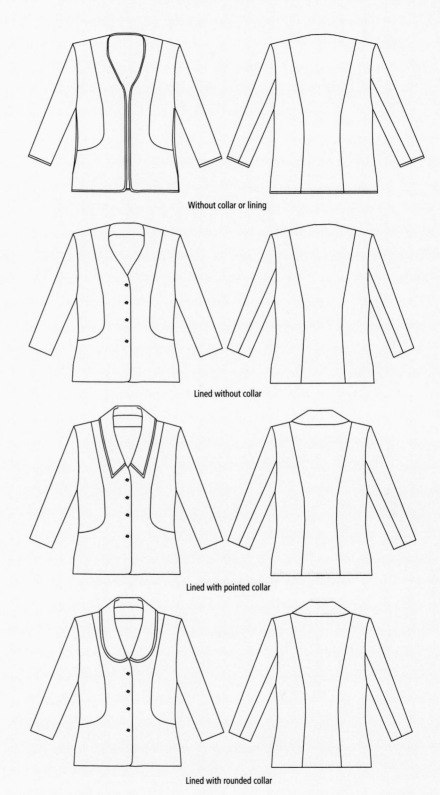

Without collar or lining

Lined without collar

Lined with pointed collar

Lined with rounded collar

THE UNLINED JACKET

Beautiful even when worn as a basic throw-on jacket, the unlined version is the simplest style to make. There are no buttons or buttonholes and no facings or interfacing. Choose a lightweight flowing fabric, such as rayon batik, silk, cotton, polyester fleece, or wool jersey.

Step 1   With right sides facing, sew the pocket bag to the front along the upper pocket edge, between the notches. Backstitch at each notch.

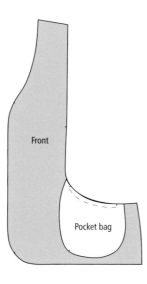

Step 3   Understitch the pocket bag to the seam allowances. Press the pocket bag to the inside.

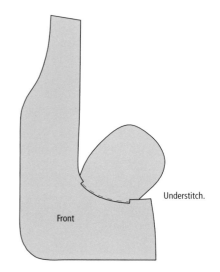

Step 2   Starting at the notch, clip the seam allowances to the stitching to allow for greater flexibility in the curve.

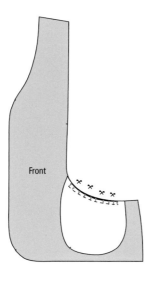

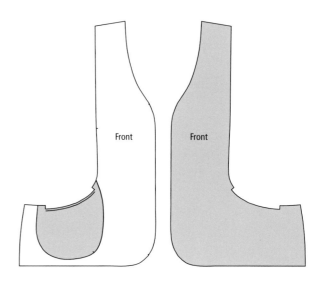

Step 4   Here's the trick to constructing the hidden pockets in the Simple Slimming Jacket: Sew the seam that attaches the front to the side front in three steps. First, with right sides facing, and matching notches, pin the front to the side front from shoulder to pocket dot. Stitch in place, stopping at the pocket dot. Backstitch.

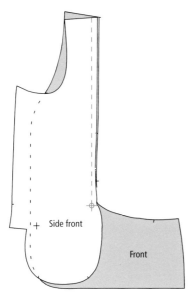

Side front

Front

Step 5   Next, flip the pocket extension to face the pocket bag. Pin, matching the notch and dots. Stitch around the pocket, stopping and backstitching at each dot.

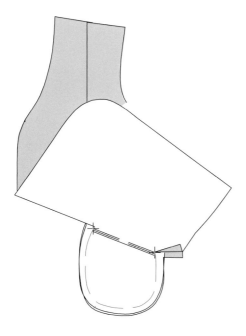

Step 6   Stitch from the side seam to pocket dot.

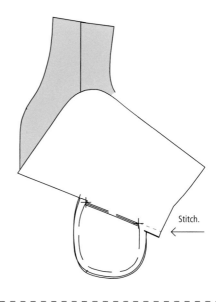

Stitch.

Step 7   Now that your seam is complete, serge the raw edges from the shoulder all the way around the pocket bag. Press the seam flat and then toward the CF. Press the pocket seam down.

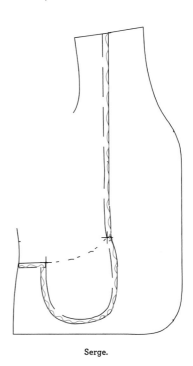

Serge.

Step 8 With right sides facing and matching notches, pin the back to the side back pieces. Stitch the seams. Serge or zigzag-stitch the raw edges. Press the seam allowances toward the CB.

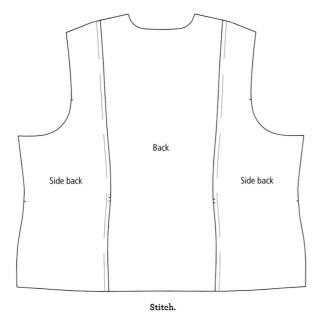

Stitch.

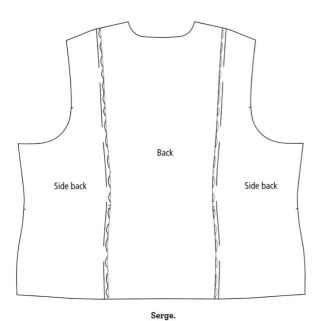

Serge.

Step 9 With right sides facing and matching princess seams, pin the front to the back at the shoulders. Stitch in place. Serge or zigzag-stitch to clean-finish the seams. Press the seam allowances toward the back.

Stitch.

Serge.

Step 10 Next, sew the side seams. With right sides facing and matching notches, pin side front to side back. Stitch in place. Clean-finish the seams. Press the seam allowances toward the back.

Step 11 With right sides facing, sew the upper sleeve to the under sleeve. Clean-finish the seams. Press the seam allowances toward the under sleeve.

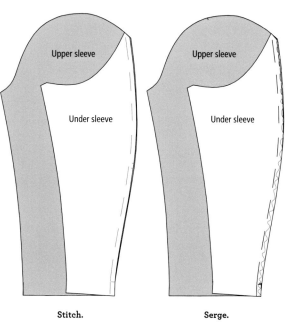

Stitch.   Serge.

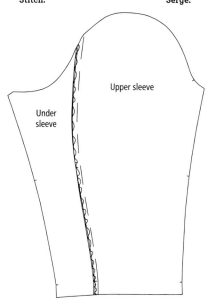

Press.

Step 12 Clean-finish the raw edge along the wrist of the sleeve. Then press up a 1¼" (3 cm) hem on the sleeves, but do not stitch.

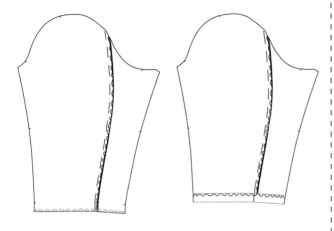

Step 13 With right sides facing and matching notches, stitch the underarm seams. Clean-finish the seams. Press the seam allowances toward the upper sleeve.

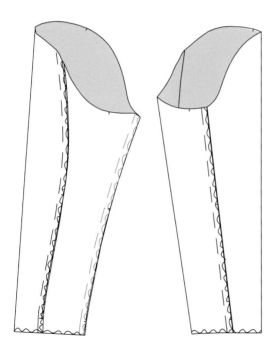

Step 14 Turn up the sleeve hem to its finished position and machine-stitch in place.

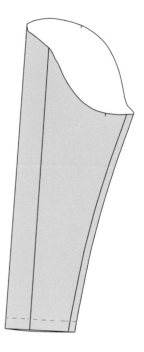

Step 15 On each sleeve cap, machine-baste with a long stitch just inside the seam allowance, from the front sleeve seam, over the cap, past the shoulder notch and to the back sleeve seam.

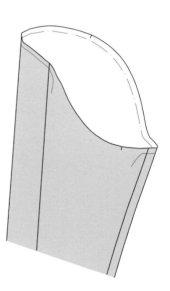

Step 16   Gather the basting stitches to form a softly shaped sleeve cap. With right side up, drape the sleeve cap over a tailor's ham. Hold your steam iron over the cap and shrink out as much of the puckering as possible. Try to make the sleeve cap softly rounded and smooth.

- -

Step 17   Pin the sleeve into the armscye with right sides facing. Match the notches as follows:

- Shoulder notch at the top of the cap to the shoulder seam
- Back sleeve seam to the double notch on the back armhole
- Underarm notch to the side seam
- Front sleeve seam to the front sleeve notch

- -

Step 18   Stitch in place. Double-stitch the seam for reinforcement. Remove the basting threads. Serge to clean-finish the armhole seam.

- -

Step 19   Next, add shoulder pads to give the jacket soft structure. For the unlined jacket, you might want to cover the shoulder pads with the same fabric as your jacket. Place each shoulder pad onto a square of fabric that can be folded into a triangle. Pin at each corner, and then stitch around the packet. Clean-finish the seam.

- -

Step 20   Try on the jacket. Carefully place the shoulder pads so they extend into the sleeve slightly and are even with the armhole seam allowance. Pin the shoulder pads in place from the outside of the garment. Hand-tack in place first at the shoulder seam near the neck and then along the armhole seam allowance.

- -

Step 21   Clean-finish the outer edges of the jacket. Press up ⅜" (1 cm) to the wrong side, all the way around the jacket. A precise way to do this is to first machine-stitch a basting line using your sewing machine stitch guide.

> **A light shoulder pad adds support** to a jacket shoulder. A slimming trick is to extend the shoulder pad out slightly into the sleeve. The sleeve will skim smoothly past the curve of the upper arm.

Press Like a Pro

With the fabric right side up, place a tailor's ham beneath the jacket's underarm. Lift the sleeve up and, with your fingers, feel that the seam allowances are aiming into the sleeve and not toward the jacket. With a damp press cloth, top-press the underarm seam only. Work in small increments, and let the fabric cool before moving.

With the fabric right side up, place the sleeve cap on the ham. As before, feel with your fingers that the seam allowances are aimed in toward the sleeve. Steam the cap by holding your iron over (but not touching) the fabric along the seamline. Finger-press the seamline, making a soft roll in the cap. Let the fabric cool and the sleeve roll set before moving the sleeve from the hem.

Step 22   Topstitch from the right side evenly around the jacket.

More Style Options

IF THE PATTERN FITS, keep wearing it! Here are some simple design ideas that will help you create some jacket variations to add interest and style to complete your mix-and-match wardrobe.

The Simple Slimming Jacket in corduroy, lined and worn with cotton blend blouse (page 62) and cotton blend print skirt (page 52)

Lined and Tailored Jacket

The tailored version of this jacket is perfect for business events and for dressier occasions. It's just as easy to make as the unlined version. There are just a few more steps—well worth the extra effort!

Interfacing gives a tailored garment resilience and staying power. Choose an interfacing that suits the weight and drape of your fabric. If in doubt, choose a lighter-weight interfacing rather than one that is heavy and stiff.

Step 1   Apply preshrunk fusible interfacing, according to the manufactur-er's instruction, to the wrong sides of the garment pieces listed:

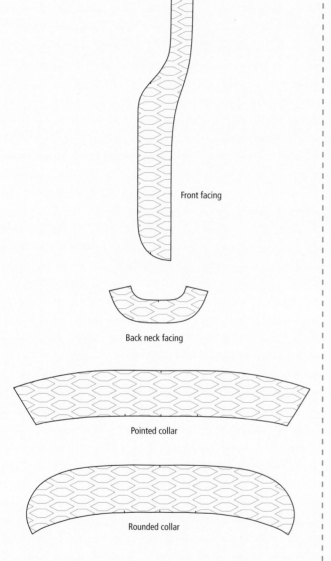

Front facing

Back neck facing

Pointed collar

Rounded collar

Step 2   Follow steps 1 through 8 for the unlined version of the jacket (pages 108–110). Because you have the lining, you won't need to serge the raw edges of the seams. You might want to serge the raw edge of the pocket bag for reinforcement, however. With the exception of the pocket pieces, press all the seam allowances first flat, then open.

Step 3   Follow the instructions for the sleeves for the unlined jacket, steps 11 through 18 (pages 111–113). When pressing the seams on the back, however, press the seam allowances open. Because the sleeve will be lined, do not topstitch the hem in place.

Step 4   Follow the instructions for the shoulder pads for the unlined jacket (page 113). Because the pads will be sandwiched between the jacket and lining, you don't need to cover the pads with fabric.

Step 5   Next, construct the jacket lining. With right sides together, stitch the dart closed on the front lining. Then press the seam allowances toward the side.

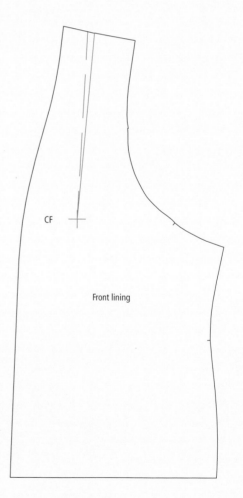

CF

Front lining

Step 6 On the back lining, stitch the CB seam from the hem to the fold. Press the seam to one side. Form the CB pleat by matching the notches at the neckline. Press the fold to the one side. Baste in place at the neck edge.

Step 7 With right sides facing and notches matching, sew the side back lining pieces to the back lining. Press the seam allowances to one side.

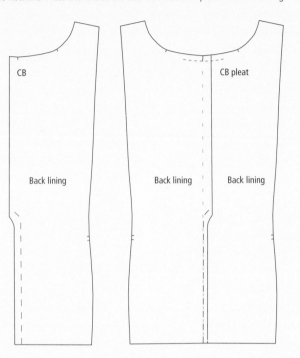

Step 8 With right sides facing and matching notches, stitch the lining side seams. Press the seam allowances toward the back.

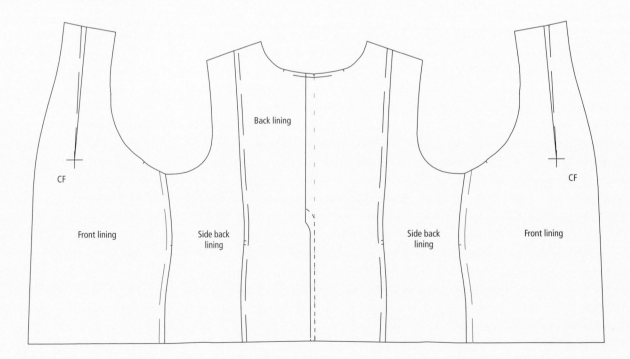

Step 9 Join the front lining to the back lining by stitching along the shoulder seams, right sides facing, matching princess seams. Press the seam allowances toward the back.

Back lining

Side back lining

Side back lining

Step 10 For the sleeve lining, repeat the steps for the unlined jacket (pages 111–113). Because the seams will all be encased by the lining, you don't need to finish the raw edges. On one sleeve lining, leave the back seam unstitched for 5" to 6" (12.5 to 15 cm). You will use the opening to turn the jacket right side out.

Step 11 Pin the sleeve lining into the lining armscye with right sides together. Match the notches. Stitch in place. Double-stitch the seam for reinforcement. Remove the basting threads.

To **"set" your stitching,** press seams flat first, then open. This technique from the tailor's workroom will ensure a smooth, flat finish to your seams. Lining seam allowances need only to be pressed flat, then to one side.

Step 12 With right sides facing, join the front facings to the back neck facing along the shoulder seams. Press the seam allowances flat first, then open.

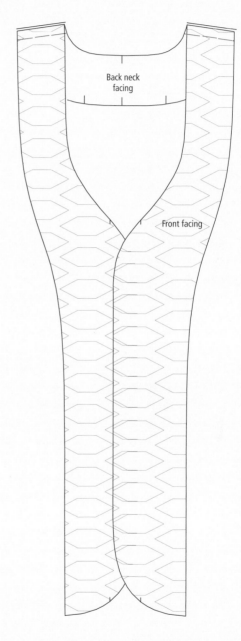

Back neck facing

Front facing

Step 13 With right sides together, matching notches and raw edges, sew the facing to the lining. Press the seam allowances toward the lining. Continue with the instructions to add a collar if you choose to make one. If you are not making a collar, go to step 19, and continue with the instructions for the facing/lining.

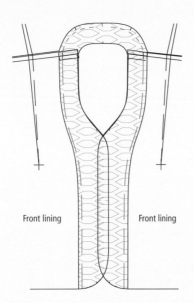

Front lining   Front lining

Step 14 If you are making a collar, choose either the pointed or rounded variation.

Step 15 With right sides facing, stitch together the upper and under collars, leaving the neckline edge open.

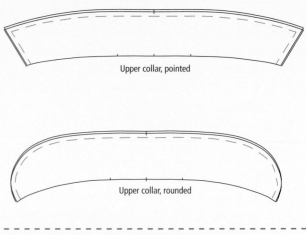

Upper collar, pointed

Upper collar, rounded

Step 16 Turn the collar to its finished position and press.

Step 17 To finish the collar, edgestitch from the top side around the outside edge.

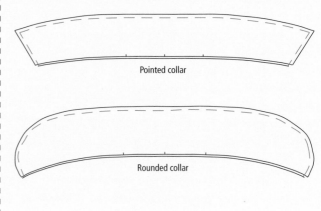

Pointed collar

Rounded collar

Understitching

For a truly professional finish that ensures facings don't peek out, understitch the seam allowances to the facings along the CF and neckline and to the lining along the hem edge. You should understitch before pressing the seams. Understitching is tricky because you need to work inside the bag of the lining from the opening of the underarm seam. You might want to have a second opening in the side seam of the lining—larger than the one in the sleeve lining. Position the jacket inside out

onto the sewing machine bed. With the open lining underarm seam or side seam as your point of entry, line up the lower edge of the facing under the machine presser foot. Use your fingers to be sure that the seam allowance is sitting under the facing. Begin sewing, keeping your stitches close—about ⅛" (3 mm)—to the original seamline. Understitch around the jacket opening. When complete, turn the jacket right side out through the open lining seam. Press as described in step 20.

Step 18   With right sides together, pin the finished collar to the right side of the jacket. Match the notches to the CB and shoulder seams. Match the finished ends of the collar to the CF notches on the jacket. Machine-baste from the CF notch to the CF notch.

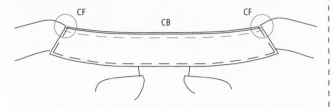

Step 19   Pin the facing/lining unit to the jacket, right sides together. Pin in place, matching seams. Stitch around the entire outside edge of the jacket.

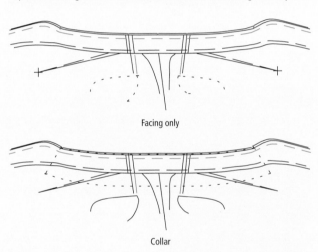

Facing only

Collar

Step 20   Understitch if desired (see sidebar, below left). Set the stitching by pressing the seam flat. Turn the jacket right side out by pulling through the open underarm seam in the sleeve lining. Lay the jacket flat, and press the seams to a smooth finish. Take your time, working in small increments and smoothing curves with your fingers. It's helpful to work with a damp press cloth or a Teflon iron shoe.

Step 21   Anchors are important little hand-tacked stitches that keep your jacket and lining neatly together. Turn the jacket inside out. With a needle and thread, hand-tack the lining seam allowance to the garment seam allowance at the back neck facing and shoulder seams. The sleeve hems and underarms will be anchored later.

Step 22   With garment right side out, put on the jacket. Fold the sleeve and sleeve lining hems up as they would appear in the finished garment. Hold the edge of the lining and the sleeve in place as you pull the sleeve inside out.

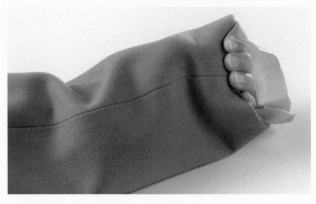

Step 23   Here's where that little opening in the sleeve lining comes into action. Reach inside the opening, and find the edge of both the jacket sleeve hem and the sleeve lining hem.

Step 24   Grasp the two edges between thumb and finger. Hold both and pull them back through the opening of the sleeve lining.

Step 25   Place a pin to hold the two edges together.

Step 26   Stitch the sleeve lining to the garment, matching the cut edges and stitching around the sleeve at the wrist edge.

Step 27   Hand-stitch or machine-tack the hem at each seam allowance.

Pressing Tools

Here are some tools that will help you do a great job pressing your tailored jacket. **Steam iron:** Choose a heavy iron with a generous reservoir for water. **Press cloth:** Lay the cloth onto the right side of your fabric to prevent shine, scorch, or other heat damage. You can buy specially woven press cloths from notion retailers or make your own using fabric made of natural fibers. I like lightweight material in 100 percent cotton or linen. **Teflon shoe or slipper:** A convenient alternative to a press cloth, and made from a patented material, these soleplates slip onto your iron like a shoe and prevent scorch and shine. **Tailor's ham:** This firmly packed cushion is shaped like a ham. Place a ham underneath your garment when pressing the seams along curves. **Sleeve board:** You can slide this mini ironing board inside sleeves and pant legs. **Clapper:** The clapper is a rounded block of hardwood used to form sharp creases in heavy fabric. Press the bulky edge of your garment with the iron. Lift the iron and, with the other hand, immediately pound, or clap, the pressed area with the clapper. The pounding speeds the removal of steam from the fabric. You can also press down with the clapper for a longer period than is safe with an iron, avoiding heat and steam damage to your garment while still getting a good hard press.

Step 28   In the same way, tack the seam allowance of the sleeve lining to the garment at the underarm and shoulder seams. Reach into the opening of the sleeve lining, and turn the sleeve to see the finished hem.

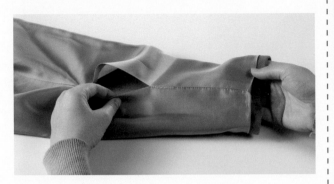

Step 29   Close the sleeve lining with a long machine stitch.

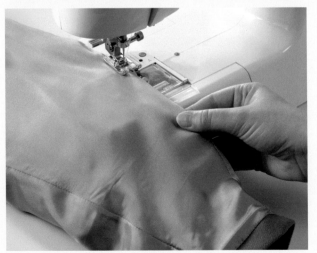

Step 30   Pull the sleeve right side out. Doesn't that look professional!

Step 31   Turn the jacket right side out, and give it a final light press. Because you've been pressing with each step, this final press is really just a touch-up to remove surface wrinkles.

Step 32   Machine-stitch four buttonholes in place on the right front. Sew buttons in place along the left front.

The Right Closure

It's important to choose the right closure. Sometimes, your fabric—like the metallic woven in the jacket at left—has so much "wow" that buttons would take away from its beauty. Make the final decision about your closures after you've completed the garment. This way, you can try on the garment and experiment a bit to see what you like best. The ensemble on the left looked best with the jacket simply left open to reveal the complementary separates. A pretty brooch works as a closure for the turquoise jacket at right.

This silver ensemble looks best with the jacket left open.

A shell-shaped brooch is the perfect closure for this corduroy jacket.

51 Mix-and-Match Wardrobe Choices

HERE ARE FIFTY-ONE DIFFERENT OUTFITS for your wardrobe, all made from the four patterns included in this book! Mix and match separates—and add new colors and fabrics—to build a closet full of flattering garments for all the occasions and activities of your life. You'll never again say, "I have nothing to wear!"

**Long-Sleeve Blouse with Collar /
Classic Pants**

**Striped Long-Sleeve Blouse with
Collar / Classic Pants**

**Cap-Sleeve Blouse /
Classic Pants**

**Long-Sleeve Blouse with Collar /
Classic Pants**

**Plaid Cap-Sleeve Blouse with Collar /
Classic Pants**

**Wool Flannel Jacket / Long-Sleeve Blouse
with Collar / Classic Pants**

Wool Flannel Jacket /Striped Long-Sleeve
Blouse with Collar / Classic Pants

Wool Flannel Jacket / Cap-Sleeve Blouse /
Classic Pants

Wool Flannel Jacket / Long-Sleeve
Blouse with Collar / Classic Pants

Wool Flannel Jacket / Plaid Cap-Sleeve
Blouse with Collar / Classic Pants

Silver Jacket / Long-Sleeve Blouse with
Collar / Classic Pants

Long-Sleeve Blouse with Collar /
Satin Skirt

Chiffon Shawl / Long-Sleeve Blouse with
Collar / Satin Skirt

Chiffon Shawl / Long-Sleeve Blouse
with Collar / Classic Pants

Silver Jacket / Long-Sleeve Blouse
with Collar / Satin Skirt

Plaid Cap-Sleeve Blouse with Collar /
Plaid Skirt

Long-Sleeve Blouse with Plaid Piping /
Lined Capri Pants

Plaid Cap-Sleeve Blouse with Collar /
Lined Capri Pants

Long-Sleeve Blouse with Plaid Piping /
Plaid Skirt

Wool Flannel Jacket / Plaid Cap-Sleeve
Blouse with Collar / Plaid Skirt

Wool Flannel Jacket / Long-Sleeve Blouse
with Plaid Piping / Lined Capri Pants

Wool Flannel Jacket / Plaid Cap-Sleeve Blouse with Collar / Lined Capri Pants

Wool Flannel Jacket / Long-Sleeve Blouse with Plaid Piping / Plaid Skirt

Cap-Sleeve Blouse / Plaid Skirt

Cap-Sleeve Blouse / Lined Capri Pants

Long-Sleeve Blouse with Collar / Plaid Skirt

Striped Long-Sleeve Blouse with Collar / Lined Capri Pants

Wool Flannel Jacket / Cap-Sleeve Blouse /
Plaid Skirt

Wool Flannel Jacket / Cap-Sleeve Blouse /
Lined Capri Pants

Chiffon Shawl / Plaid Cap-Sleeve Blouse
with Collar / Plaid Skirt

Wool Flannel Jacket / Long-Sleeve Blouse
with Collar / Plaid Skirt

Wool Flannel Jacket / Striped Long-Sleeve
Blouse with Collar / Lined Capri Pants

Chiffon Shawl / Long-Sleeve Blouse with
Collar / Plaid Skirt

Silver Jacket / Cap-Sleeve Blouse with Collar / Plaid Skirt

Silver Jacket / Long-Sleeve Blouse with Collar / Plaid Skirt

Long-Sleeve Blouse with Collar / Corduroy Pants

Long-Sleeve Blouse with Collar /
Corduroy Pants

Cap-Sleeve Blouse /
Corduroy Pants

Corduroy Jacket / Long-Sleeve Blouse with
Collar / Corduroy Pants

Corduroy Jacket / Long-Sleeve Blouse
with Collar / Corduroy Pants

Corduroy Jacket / Cap-Sleeve
Blouse / Corduroy Pants

Long-Sleeve Blouse with Collar /
Summer Print Skirt

Cap-Sleeve Blouse / Summer Print Skirt

Corduroy Jacket / Long-Sleeve Blouse with Collar / Summer Print Skirt

**Batik Cap-Sleeve Blouse with Collar /
Batik Skirt**

Cap-Sleeve Blouse / Batik Skirt

**Batik Jacket / Cap-Sleeve Blouse /
Batik Skirt**

**Batik Cap-Sleeve Blouse with Collar /
Capri Pants**

Cap-Sleeve Blouse / Capri Pants

**Batik Jacket / Cap-Sleeve Blouse /
Capri Pants**

Fabric Requirements and Measurements

These fabric measurements have no allowance for shrinkage, matching, or lengthening. Be sure to check the Finished Garment Measurements Chart and Body Measurement Chart (page 33) to determine if you need to lengthen or shorten the pattern for your height. To lengthen, multiply the increase in length by two to calculate the additional fabric you'll need.

To avoid problems with shrinkage, before cutting your fabric, pretreat the entire length in the same way that you will clean the garment later. Ask the fabric seller about the expected shrinkage, and add that percentage to the yardage (meterage) in the Fabric Requirements Chart.

Flirty Skirt

Fabric Requirements
The Flirty Skirt pattern is just one piece that is cut six times. You can cut the pieces on the straight of grain or, for an even more fluid effect, cut the six pieces on the bias. If you are cutting the skirt on the bias, open the fabric to a single layer.

For skirt cut on the straight of grain
Size: 14 to 24
Width: 45" to 60" (114.5 to 152.5 cm)
Length: 2½ yd. (2.3 m)

For skirt cut on the bias
Size: 14 to 24
Width: 45" (114.5 cm)
Length: 3⅞ yd. (3.6 m)
Width: 54" to 60" (137 to 152.5 cm)
Length: 2⅜ yd. (2.2 m)

Notions
thread
2 yd. (1.8 m) of ¾" (2 cm)-wide sport-style elastic

Finished Garment Measurement
Length: 25" (63.5 cm)

Shapely Blouse

Fabric Requirements

Size: 14 to 24
Width: 45" to 60" wide (114.5 to 152.5 cm)
Length:

Blouse View	Yards	Meters
Faced neckline with long sleeve	2⅞	2.5
Faced neckline with cap sleeve	2⅓	2
Collar with cap sleeve	2⅞	2.5
Collar with long sleeve	3⅜	3

Notions

thread
five ¾" (2 cm) buttons
1 yd. (1 m) of lightweight fusible interfacing

Finished Garment Measurements

SIZE	14		16		18		20		22		24	
	in	*cm*	*in*	*cm*	*in*	*cm*	*in*	*cm*	*in*	*cm*	*in*	*cm*
Length, center back to hem	23⅜	59.5	23½	59.5	23½	59.5	23⅝	60	23⅝	60	23¾	60
Length of long sleeve	20¾	53	20⅞	53.5	20⅞	53.5	21⅛	54	21¼	54	21⅜	54
Length of cap sleeve	5⅛	13	5⅛	13.5	5¼	13.5	5¼	13.5	5⅜	14	5⅜	14

Classic Fly-Front Pants

Fabric Requirements

Size: 14 to 24

Width: 54" and 60" (137 and 152.5 cm)

Length: 2½ yd. (2.5 m)

Notions

thread

1" (2.5 cm)-wide sport elastic

7" (18 cm) zipper

½ yd. (0.5 m) fusible interfacing

Optional: If you choose to have one side of your pocket cut in lining fabric, you will need ½ yd. (0.5 m) of lining.

Elastic

Size	in	cm
14	7	18
16	7½	19
18	8	20.5
20	8½	21.5
22	9	23
24	9½	24

Finished Garment Measurements

SIZE	14		16		18		20		22		24	
	in	cm	in	cm	in	cm	in	cm	in	cm	in	cm
Outseam (waist to hem along the side seam)	37	94	37⅛	94.5	37⅜	95	37⅜	95	37⅝	95.5	38⅛	97
Width of hem (laid flat)	9¼	23.5	9½	24	9¾	25	10	25.5	10¼	26	10½	26.5

Simple Slimming Jacket

Fabric Requirements

Size: 14 to 24

Width: 45" to 60" (114.5 to 152.5 cm)

Length:

Jacket View	Yards	Meters
Jacket without collar	2⅞	2.6
Jacket with collar	3½	3.2
Lining	2¾	2.5
Interfacing		
Lined Jacket without collar	⅞	0.8
Lined Jacket with collar	1¼	1.1

Notions

thread

four ¾" (2 cm) buttons

Finished Garment Measurements

Length center back to hem: 23½" (59.5 cm)

Length of sleeve: 21½" (54.5 cm)

Glossary of Sewing Terms

Every area of specialization has its own terminology—and sewing is no different. Throughout the book, you'll frequently find these common sewing terms and abbreviations.

CB: Center back

CF: Center front

Bias: Any line diagonal to the fabric's crosswise and lengthwise grains

Backstitching: Reverse stitching that secures the beginning and end of each seam

Bartack: A medium-width zigzag stitch that reinforces a corner or area that receives stress

Double stitching: Two rows of stitching on the right side of the garment, on top of a seam allowance. The first row is stitched close to the seam and is then repeated about ¼" (6 mm) from the first row of topstitching. The stitch length should be medium to long.

Edgestitch: Straight stitching ⅛" (3 mm) from the finished edge to prevent the edges from stretching or rolling

Grading: Trimming the seam allowances in staggered widths to eliminate extra bulk

Left side: The pattern piece that falls on the left side of the garment when worn

Muslin: A plain weave fabric of cotton or linen; also a test garment that is made with inexpensive fabric to check the fit of a pattern

Notches: Notches that are marked on fabric with a tiny clip into the edge of the piece; this marking technique is used in the ready-to-wear industry and provides greater accuracy than conventional home-sewing notches. (As a substitute, mark fabric that is loosely woven or unravels easily with a disappearing fabric marker.)

Pressing: Setting each seam with a steam iron in an up-and-down motion

Right side: The pattern piece that falls on the right side of the garment when worn

Seam allowances: The amount of fabric from the stitching line to the raw edge; seam allowances on these patterns are ⅜" (1 cm) unless otherwise indicated on the tissue

Selvage: The tightly woven edge that runs the length of the fabric, parallel to the straight of grain

Serging: A method of **clean-finishing** the raw edges with stitches made on a serger, a machine that seams, trims, and overcasts raw edges in one step. Zigzag-stitching on a sewing machine is an alternative to serging.

Stitch-in-the-ditch: Stitching on the right side of the garment, sewn in the valley or "ditch" formed by the seamline

Staystitching: Stitching that reinforces and prevents stretching and distortion in curved pieces such as crotches, armscyes, and necklines during construction

Straight of grain: The orientation of the yarns in a woven fabric that run parallel to the selvage

Straight stitch: Stitching in a straight line with a stitch length of 9 to 12 stitches per inch (2.5 cm)

Understitch: Rolling the seam allowance slightly toward the facing and stitching the facing to the seam allowance. This technique stops pockets and facings from rolling to the outside of your garment.

Glossary of Fabrics

Cotton, flax (linen), rayon, silk, and **wool** are all natural fibers. Natural fibers "breathe" and so have natural cooling and warming properties. Although my preference is for natural fibers, there are some very good synthetics now available that offer many of the qualities of natural fibers.

Polyester is a synthetic fiber that is popular because it does not wrinkle like cotton and linen. I often use it for eveningwear. You will also see polyester blended with natural fibers. The beauty of this particular blend is that you receive the benefits of both—a breathable cotton with polyester's resistance to wrinkles.

Spandex, often referred to by its trade name, Lycra, is an elastic fiber that is often blended into many of the new fabrics to give them stretch. The higher the percentage of spandex in the fabric, the greater the amount of stretch. Typically, 3 percent of spandex in a cotton or wool fabric will be more than enough to make a very comfortable blouse or pair of pants. Check the fiber content on the manufacturer's label on the end of the fabric bolt. This label also provides care instructions.

The names *broadcloth, challis, chiffon, corduroy, crepe, flannel, interlock, jersey, satin, tweed,* and *twill* refer to the process of weaving or knitting the fabric. These fabrics can be manufactured from either natural or synthetic fibers.

Broadcloth: A closely woven fabric with fine ribs commonly used for shirts and blouses.

Challis: A soft, lightweight, plain-weave fabric that is often delicately printed and very nice for skirts, blouses, and shawls.

Chiffon: A plain-weave fabric that is very light, transparent, and drapable; often used for overskirts and shawls.

Corduroy: A durable cut-pile fabric with narrow or wide wales (raised ribs or ridges). This fabric is often used for pants and jackets.

Crepe: A fabric with a dull, crinkly surface created from tightly twisted yarns. Depending on its weight, it can be used for pants, blouses, skirts, and jackets.

Flannel: A soft, plain- or twill-weave cloth with a brushed surface, made in many fibers and weights. Cotton flannel is commonly used for sleepwear. Wool flannel is a popular fabric for pants and jackets.

Interlock: A closely knit, smooth, stretchy double knit with an identical surface on both sides of the fabric. Cotton interlock is used for T-shirts. Wool interlock is used for skirts, dresses, and jackets.

Jersey: A knitted fabric with a smooth, dull finish that is elastic and drapable. It tends to be lighter in weight than interlock and is used for dresses, skirts, tops, and pants.

Satin: A lustrous fabric with floating surface yarns that give the right side of the fabric a shine. The wrong side of the fabric has a dull finish. Satin is usually made in polyester or silk for special occasions but sometimes from cotton and wool for shirts, pants, and jackets.

Tweed: A rough-surfaced fabric with mixed color slubs of yarn that form a speckled effect on a fibrous surface. The colorful slubs make this fabric a versatile choice for jackets and coats because the garments can be easily matched to pants and skirts in different colors.

Twill: A strong resilient fabric with a subtle angled texture. Lightweight twills are used for shirts, and heavier-weight twills for pants and jeans.

Sources of Supply

THE WOOLS IN THE FALL/ WINTER GROUPING:

The Woolen Mill Store
8550 SE McLoughlin Boulevard
Portland, OR 97222
1-866-865-9285
http://thewoolenmillstore.blogspot
.com

THE COORDINATED COTTONS IN THE SPRING/SUMMER GROUPING:

Troy Corporation
2701 North Normandy Ave
Chicago, IL 60707
www.troy-corp.com

Ask for this wholesaler's fabrics when shopping at your favorite fabric retail location.

THE RAYON BATIKS IN THE BATIK CRUISE GROUPING:

The Batik Butik
www.batikbutik.com

Ask for this wholesaler's fabrics when shopping at your favorite fabric retail location.

THE SILVER AND GRAY COORDINATES:

The fabrics for the core and special occasion groupings came from the author's personal stash of fabrics collected over time and stored beneath her cutting table.

THE SILK AND COTTON SWATCHES IN THE DESIGN EXERCISES:

Exotic Silks
www.exoticsilks.com

JB Silks
www.jbsilks.com

Télio
www.telio.com

Troy Corporation
www.troy-corp.com

Ask for these wholesalers' fabrics when shopping at your favorite fabric retail location.

PATTERN-MAKING TOOLS, PRESSING TOOLS, AND SEWING SUPPLIES:

Joanne's Creative Notions (Canada)
1-800-811-6611 or 905-453-1805
http://joannescreativenotions.com/
store/index.php

A Great Notion (Canada)
www.agreatnotion.com
1-800-309-2829 or 604-575-9023

Clotilde (USA)
www.clotilde.com
1-800-772-2891

Nancy's Notions (USA)
www.nancysnotions.com
1-800-833-0690

Perpetual Patterns (Australia)
http://perpetualpatterns.com.au
+61 (03) 9809 2585

INSTRUCTIONAL VIDEOS TO SEE PRESSING AND TAILORING TECHNIQUES IN ACTION:

Constructing the Princess Seamed Blazer with Kathleen Cheetham and Vija Anca, DVD and VHS, available from www.petitepluspatterns.com

Fearless Pressing with Cecelia Podolak, DVD and VHS, available from www.ceceliapodolak.com

Japanese Tailoring with Judy Barlup, DVD, available from www.unique techniques.com

Index

About the Author

Kathleen Cheetham's mission is to help every woman—no matter her size—look fabulous. She owns a woman's custom tailoring business and also teaches classes on fitting and design. Her articles have appeared in *Threads* magazine, and her line of patterns has been featured in *Sew News, Threads, Australian Stitches,* and *Sewing World.* She teaches workshops and sells her pattern line at trade shows throughout the United States and Canada. She lives in Sointula, British Columbia. Visit her at her website, www.petitepluspatterns.com.

"Kathleen not only gives us patterns that fit and excellent construction techniques, she also adds personal style, wardrobe planning, and fitting and sewing instruction. Packaged with four versatile patterns, this book has everything you need! Her writing style is delightful, the perfect blend of artistic and technical, professional and friendly. Whether you are a plus size or not, this book belongs in your sewing library."

—**Judy Barlup**, teacher, author, and founder of *Unique Techniques*

"Kathleen Cheetham has done a good job of simplifying the pattern alterations that are often needed for the fuller figure. The step-by-step construction photos are well done and easy to follow."

—**Sandra Betzina**, author of *Power Sewing* and host of online sewing classes at sandrabetzina.com

"Kathleen reminds me of how Tim Gunn tells the designers on Project Runway, 'Make it work!' She does just that. *Perfect Plus* is a gem, certain to become a classic reference book—no matter what your figure size. The clothes are so simple, so interesting. Four stars, a big YES!"

—**Marcy Tilton**, pattern designer, fiber artist, and creativity coach

"Great concept! An annotated pattern collection in a book. This is way more than just a book on style, fitting, figure flattery, or pattern variations. It's a complete action plan for frustrated sewers. Love it!"

—**David Page Coffin**, former editor of *Threads* magazine and author of *Shirtmaking*

"There are so many practical tips that I wanted to immediately go to my fabric stash and begin sewing. Everything's here and well organized—including a daily schedule to help you find time for sewing!"

—**Ce Podolak**, pattern designer and author of *Easy Guide to Sewing Jackets*

"If you follow Kathleen's advice, you'll end up with the perfect wardrobe—and clothes that fit, flatter, and coordinate. Every sewer needs this book!"

—**Susan Khalje**, author of *Linen and Cotton* and *Bridal Couture* and host of DIY.net's "Sew Much More"